FORT DIX STOCKADE

FORT DIX STOCKADE

OUR PRISON CAMP
NEXT DOOR

BY
JOAN CROWELL

Links

NEW YORK   LONDON

Published by Links Books
33 West 60 Street, New York 10023 and
78 Newman Street, London W. 1
Distributed by Quick Fox, Inc.
33 West 60 Street, New York 10023 and
Quick Fox Limited, 40 Nugget Avenue, Unit 11,
Agincourt, Ontario, Canada

First Printing
Standard Book Numbers:
0-8256-3027-4 softcover edition
0-8256-3035-5 hardcover edition

Printed in the United States of America

Designed by Uli

For:

Bill Brakefield
Tom Catlow
Terry Klug
Jeff Russell
Carlos Rodriguez Torres

and
Rowland Watts
without whose help
and guidance
this book would never be

ACKNOWLEDGMENTS

To John Simon and Hilary Maddux of Random House for suffering with me through several versions of this manuscript.

To a great array of typists, too numerous to mention, for transcribing tapes and notes.

To the Workers Defense League: Clariss Ritter Catlow, Fred Gross, Bill Pankratius and Marilyn S. Brook for their time, patience and help.

To Joe Pierpont for introducing me to Rowland Watts.

To lawyers Fred Cohn, Henry DiSuvero, Judith Vladeck and Tim Coulter for giving me hours of their time and letting me tape their thoughts.

To Beth Reisen, Sam Karp, Margaret Meister, Herb Dreyer, Kathy Russell and Saul Shapiro for filling me in on the Coffeehouse and *Shakedown*.

To Mark Amsterdam, Arpiar Saunders, Joseph Remcho, Bart Lubow, Reber Boult for their help in gathering information on conditions in stockades and brigs here and overseas.

To the secretaries of Senator Birch Bayh and Congressman Jonathan Bingham for furnishing me with needed materials.

To Leroi Conley, Joe LeBanc and Andy Stapp for added material on the demonstration.

To Colonel Moon and Sergeant Vaughn, Reporter Larry Jackson, Mike Uhal of the War Crimes Bureau for furnishing materials on PCF.

To William F. Caron and Scott Thomas for the most recent materials on conditions at Fort Dix.

To Robert Sherrill, whom I've never met but whose book was an inspiration.

To Danny Moses of Links Books for having the faith and courage to let this manuscript see the light of day.

Most especially to Carol R. Anderson for typing, retyping and then again typing the many versions of this book.

And to my husband, David, for just being and for giving me the title of Chapter 5.

My thanks and deep gratitude
Joan Crowell

CONTENTS

FOREWORD

I'm a novelist, poet, freelance writer, and the mother of five grown children. My family and I (along with countless others) were totally opposed to the war in Vietnam, but it wasn't until my draft-aged son decided that under no circumstances would he be drafted that I learned, in depth, of the pain behind that decision. He went through a period of great inner conflict and soul-searching. It is one thing to oppose a policy. It is quite another thing to make a moral choice about one's own life and stand by that decision. My son was among the fortunate: he wasn't drafted and didn't have to serve time in jail, or a stockade, or flee his country. Through his experience I became increasingly sensitive to the moral anguish of a host of other young men who were not so fortunate. Young people who had never before considered life in absolute terms of morality were being forced to make a decision that was to change their lives, their thinking, and their very sense of allegiance. Adults were speaking for them or analyzing these young people, but few were letting the young speak for themselves or listening when they did. The Woodstocks, the Haight-Ashburys, the Electric Circuses of the young made the front page but youth's serious declarations went largely ignored. Responsible dissenting youth went underground or chose to make their stand behind bars.

In 1968, I set out to find these young resisters, to record in their own words their outrage at the war in Vietnam, to share with a larger American public their understanding of how American policy in Vietnam has changed the lives and the thinking of a generation. It was comparatively easy to talk to and exchange ideas with resisters in cities and communes throughout the United States, even to reach the "Crossroads Church" in Hawaii, to ferret out resisters and deserters in Canada, but, for a solid year, I found it impossible to penetrate a prison, a stockade, or brig, where so many young men were putting their lives on the line.

I approached Honey Knopp, a Counselor for the Central Committee of Conscientious Objectors who had been visiting resisters in prisons for many years; the Reverend Robert Horton who, since April of 1969, when he retired from the American Friends Service Committee, had been visiting Conscientious Objectors in federal prisons all over the country; and Lincoln

Darnell, a committed civil rights lawyer who had been working with antiwar resisters in prisons and stockades. Though each was extremely helpful and gave me many hours of his time, they were unanimous in declaring it impossible for me to interview young men behind bars and advised me to get my material second hand.

By chance, a fellow writer, the late Harvey Swados, introduced me to Joe Pierpont, then of the Workers Defense League in New York. In the course of talking to Joe about my work in progress on the "moral generation," I mentioned the difficulties I was having reaching resisters in prisons. He asked if I would like to visit the stockade at Fort Dix (New Jersey) with his boss, Rowland Watts. I leapt at the chance. Rowland needed a research secretary, and, in that capacity, I visited the stockade at Dix the very next morning.

It was June 16, 1969, a full year since I had started researching my book. Rowland Watts and I left Manhattan at 7:00 A.M. in a battered Volvo. We drove through the smells and smogs of the New Jersey Turnpike. A young Puerto Rican soldier, a drug addict who had originally joined the Army in hopes of kicking his habit, accompanied us. He had recently been AWOL and had sought Rowland's help. Even as the car moved steadily closer to the Fort Dix gate, he had not yet made his decision whether to ask for a dishonorable discharge or rejoin the Army and face the stockade. We stopped at a diner for coffee. Rowland asked the young soldier whether he had decided how he was going to plead, outlining the alternatives to him once again. The young man shook his head sadly. We sat outside together while Rowland bought candy and cigarettes for the prisoners in the stockade. The young man turned to me and told me how ashamed his family in Puerto Rico would be if he quit the Army. I wanted to say, "Don't join up again if you don't believe in this war," but I just sat, silently, feeling his deep sadness, confusion and guilt.

We drove on, passing through Wrightstown and its proud sign: FORT DIX IS AN EQUAL OPPORTUNITY EMPLOYER. Rowland turned to the young man again and very gently asked what he had decided to do. In an almost inaudible reply the soldier said that he had decided to rejoin the Army. Rowland put his arm around him and with words more of a father than of a lawyer said that he must never take narcotics again, that he, (Rowland), had been an alcoholic and that he knew he must never touch another drop. Rowland Watts was a pacifist in World War II and yet here he was, backing up this young man's decision to continue as a soldier. It was then I realized the quiet strength, the uniqueness of Rowland Watts, a lawyer who has dedicated his life to social justice but insists on the sovereign right of the individual to make his own decision.

When we reached Fort Dix we said goodbye to the soldier who was turning himself in and Rowland told him to phone should he need his assistance.

As we approached the stockade, Rowland noted with amusement that the Army had removed a huge sign reading, "OBEDIENCE TO THE LAW IS FREEDOM" from the top of the stockade gate, following the riot. I had only the vaguest idea of what he was referring to, having read of a "minor uprising" at Fort Dix in the *New York Times*. This was my first clue that the uprising was in fact a riot of major proportions. We were too rushed for Rowland to fill me in. Rowland's first appointment was with Terry Klug, one of thirty-eight prisoners accused of master-minding the stockade riot of June 5, 1969. Meeting Terry then was a shock. He was the antithesis of the stockade prisoner I had pictured: lively, impish, curly light hair, small and lithe, with the charm of a musical comedy star. The extraordinary thing about Terry was his good humor in the face of a fifty-year sentence for charges growing out of the riot and the unimaginable conditions under which he had been forced to live. Later, when I had learned what his daily life was like, the horrors he had experienced, and the brutalities he had witnessed, his cheerfulness seemed that much more remarkable. Terry was full of talk of the riot: the accusations; the sinister methods of the Army's Criminal Investigating Division; and numerous details of the riot itself. While he talked with Rowland, I wrote in a feverish scrawl. As I learned more and more of what was going on at Dix, I made a major decision: The "moral generation" book would have to wait.

On June 5, 1969 two hundred and fifty men rioted in the stockade to let the public know about the tortures, brutality, and barbarous conditions under which they were condemned to live. The irony is that to this day, so many years later, though the words FORT DIX did make the headlines of the *Daily News* newspaper and though the words Fort Dix are still in the air, the public has yet to hear of the conditions that caused the riot, the details of the riot itself, or the stories of the young men each of whom faced court-martial sentences of up to fifty years.

We can approach stockades, as one magazine editor said to me, with, "Didn't you read the stockade scenes in *From Here to Eternity?* What do you expect?" Or we can approach stockades as Rowland Watts does, as a human, caring being. In Dickens' day a "gentleman" accepted cruelty to children of the lower classes as a necessary fact of life. An intellectual swinger in our time shakes his head or fist at the "military-industrial complex" or "technological society" but accepts the dehumanizing brutality in our stockades with, "Come on, it's an Army prison, what do you expect?"

In my blackest nightmares I didn't expect to talk to men chained to chairs, not in America. I didn't and don't expect starvings and beatings of innocent young men, nor the use of leather straps, nor the forced "confessions" under our democratic form of government.

We are a silent majority, kept silent by a hushed press. We read in detail about so many disasters and brutalities for which we are not responsible, it is time we, as members of a democracy, find out in the same detail about those brutalities for which we are responsible; how we are treating our own sons in our own prison camps next door.

NONCOVERAGE BY THE ESTABLISHMENT PRESS

We are shocked by the lack of continuing coverage of the Ft. Dix riot courtmartials. Political persecution, military torture, denial of constitutional rights and due process are involved in each case.

**Signed by Bill Mauldin
Harvey Swados
Nat Hentoff
Congressman Mario Biaggi
Joan Simon***

(Telegram sent by Workers Defense League to *The New York Times, The Village Voice, The New York Post,* Dec. 5, 1969)

* now Crowell

After listening to Terry's first-hand account of the conditions in the stockade, the dimensions of the riot, and the cruelty with which the thirty-eight charged with rioting were treated, I tried to get the story out—to magazines, newspapers, radio and tv, Congressmen and Senators. After months of interviews with editors, writers, and literary agents, I was at a loss to understand the blanket of silence which covered the Dix story.

When I offered this story to executive editor, Shelly Zalasnic of *New York* magazine, he said, "The kids are at me all the time to do something on Dix." He never did. *Life* never did. *Look* never did. *Time* never did. *Newsweek* never did. *Harpers, The Atlantic, The New Yorker* never did. No major American magazine ran a story on the Fort Dix riot.

To this day no editor on *The New York Times* with whom I have spoken has a clear idea as to what went on down at Dix. Editors and writers offer a variety of explanations for this phenomenon, among them the fact that New York magazines and papers do not want to appear parochial and are more apt to cover an uprising in California than a riot "next door."

Every editor and reporter I interviewed about the lack of coverage on the Dix story would quickly assure me that there was no conspiracy involved. This initial reflexive response puzzled me since I had never entertained such an outrageous theory.

Shortly after the riot, when I first offered the Dix story to the *New York Times* Sunday Magazine section, it was flatly rejected. I was told that a *Times* daily reporter was going to cover this story. As it happened, I was in the same room with Carlos Rodriguez Torres, Jeffrey Russell and some other young men chained to their respective chairs when the *New York Times* daily reporter finally did visit Dix. He had hardly poked his nose in the door when he was forcibly ejected by armed MPs. I couldn't wait to open the next morning's *Times,* knowing that the reporter had seen the young men chained to their chairs and feeling sure that the physical ejection of the reporter alone would make a story. I searched the paper in vain.

One month later a story did appear, buried on page sixty-three of the hefty Sunday *Times.* The headline carried the skeptical tone of the article: SELF-STYLED POLITICAL PRISONERS' IN THE FORT DIX STOCKADE CHARGE ANTIWAR VIEWS INSPIRE BRUTALITY. Not until the end of the article does the reader learn that the reporter was thrown out of the room. I was there. The reporter had had no time for an "interview" with the prisoners. Angered by the piece, I sought out the *Times* reporter who was unwilling to be taped, but willing to grant a brief interview. He said, in effect, that after being expelled from the room with the chained prisoners that he had interviewed Major Casey, the Commander of the stockade. Major Casey kept referring to the "antiwar prisoners" as "punks and creeps." When asked why he (the reporter) didn't include this interview in his story he intimated that if it had been included the story would have been shelved for good. As it was he had had to keep prodding the editors to run the story at all.

Thomas A. Johnson, who covered one of the courts-martial at Fort Dix for *The New York Times,* was willing to be tape-recorded on the subject of the coverage and noncoverage of the Fort Dix riot. The following are some of his thoughts:

"Dix is sixty miles south of New York City. Circle around New York City for sixty miles and you'll be surprised the many things we don't cover. Dix, of course, is very important because they've got 55,000 young soldiers, many of whom come right out of this area. . . . I've been to Dix about four times in the last three years, each time because the military's Public Relations department suggested a story.

"The immediate system of beats does not cover the social problems of the military enlisted men. Our military writers write about hardware, about Vietnamization, about the big picture. We've got two men down there in the Pentagon and they're talking now about what the big thing is, the military, drugs in Vietnam, detoxification programs in Germany, whatever General Ochs said or did not say. It's one of the many sins of the media.

". . . As for the uprising at Fort Dix not getting out, I think basically it's the same story of any military organization, any large corporation—it's too easy to hide that kind of story. When you deal with the military you must depend upon their public relations people for the basic information.

". . . Another problem is that editors, assignment editors, are basically clerks rather than creative people. An editor sits down with six reporters and seventeen things to cover and he will cover the traditional things, the things he knows everyone else will cover. The great fear is that he will be caught short for not covering something that the opposition will be covering.

"Editors are like so many people on that level, they generally play it safe. They, (1) don't know that much and (2), they are not about to find out. They react along very traditional patterns. The truth of the matter is that Fort Dix is just one area in which we fall down. There are so few reporters who are really interested in it. . . ."

As Tom Johnson remarked, "Editors, like so many people on that level, play it safe." Though reporters granted me interviews, no senior editor of a major news magazine or newspaper would do more than speak with me abruptly over the phone.

I reached Arthur Gelb, Senior Editor of *The New York Times,* by phone. His first response to the question as to why the Fort Dix uprising had not been adequately covered by *The New York Times* was to assure me that there "was no conspiracy of silence involved." He then admitted that he had no idea that there had, in fact, been an uprising at Dix. After being handed the clipping files on Fort Dix, he came up with a story by Homer Bigart in the June 22, 1970 issue and quoted from it with some glee: "No mice were reported last week by an observer who gained entrance to the stockade. . . . The only creature stirring was a housefly circling a target of potato chips at an altitude of two feet."

I was shocked at the relish with which Arthur Gelb chose this sophomoric, snide piece to read to me over the phone. I agree with Mr. Gelb and all the senior editors with whom I've talked, that there is no conspiracy involved in the nonreportage of the Fort Dix story. Far worse than conspiracy is the complacency of these men in their swivel chairs.

Later, by accident, I learned that Homer Bigart had in fact been shown the deplorable conditions at one of the holding facilities on base that same day. He told Timothy Bunn, then a public relations officer at Fort Dix, that there was no story here: No story where men were living in a pigsty in the U.S. Army; no story where civilians are picked up off the street in New York, taken out to Dix and caged; no story where men are jailed for months on end without being charged; no story where men are treated more as animals than as human beings.* It is one thing for a reporter to decide that this story isn't big enough. It is another for a *New York Times* military expert to report a fly circling potato chips.

Tom Mathews, a reporter for *Newsweek,* went down to Fort Dix two or three times and wrote a long story which never ran in the magazine. Over the phone he said, "You're right. It wasn't covered adequately. I went down to Fort Dix with Andy Stapp of the American Servicemen's Union. I was surprised at how frankly the guards would talk about the stockade conditions." When asked for an explanation of why neither *Time* nor *Newsweek* had reported on the demonstration at Dix, the first time

* See "Afterword: The Cage," p. 143.

that civilians had ever demonstrated on an American Army base, he answered: ". . . We were very slow in catching on to what an important phenomenon the trouble with the military was. I think it's more our own stupidity. I don't think it's anything ideological. . . ."

Senior Editor Edward Kosner of *Newsweek* commented: "It (the Fort Dix demonstration) wasn't a conspicuous story in my purview. There are eight or nine stories a week: the specific gravity of the Dix story didn't register. Another consideration, a lot of things that happen close to New York don't get covered. Nothing amoral or ideological about not covering the story."

One could go along with Senior Editor Laurence I. Barrett of *Time* magazine when he claimed that the Fort Dix demonstration "was just one of so many stories that get lost;" and one could go along with reporter Leonard Levitt of *Time* magazine's New York bureau that, "Nobody took it (the Fort Dix story) very seriously;" were it not for the piece that *Time* did run on Fort Dix under the heading LAW on May 17, 1971. When all hell was going on in PCF, a holding facility, they ran the following paragraph:

> At Fort Dix, N.J., where the Army stockade was a mess last year, Lieutenant Colonel Arthur Friedman has launched dramatic reforms in line with his motto, "Firm but fair." To Friedman, a huge 240-pounder, his slogan means clean kitchens, well-trained guards and innovative programs for 446 inmates. Since he took charge 15 months ago, Friedman has started college preparatory classes, given the inmates a real drug-therapy program complete with talks by ex-addicts, and allowed selected prisoners off-base privileges.

The story of the riot and its aftermath went unreported and now a year later *Time* tells us all is "hunky-dory" in the stockade. *Time* reporters must know that you can't find out about the use of straps, the starving and brutalizing of prisoners by speaking to the Lieutenant Colonel in charge.

There was one writer at *Time* magazine who did think the Dix story important. She had written a long piece covering the civilian demonstration at Fort Dix following the riot and the subsequent indictment of "the Fort Dix Thirty-eight." The story never ran. Though preferring not to be named, she granted me a lengthy interview:

"I don't think it (not running the Dix story) was anything

calculated on their part. I just don't think that they thought it very important. News magazines are so limited in space; they have rather unwritten priorities. For some reason the editors of *Time* just couldn't be convinced that (1) there was a story there and (2) that it was an incredibly important story. . . .

". . . the establishment press isn't very well tuned in to any kind of underground activity or what they think is an underground activity or, God forbid, a radical activity.

"There is little or no investigating in the news magazines . . . ."

Fort Dix fared better in pictures than it did in words. Harvey Dinnerstein, a young artist, was commissioned by *Esquire* magazine to paint a series of paintings called "Dink Stover in Hell." The only text was a lead line which read, "For the next ten pages we're going to show you some of the things that happened to distinguish the academic year 1969-70." The painting of the demonstration at Fort Dix covered a two-page spread.

A prominent painter, known in the words of her biographer for a "deeply informed documentation of our mores and our social history," Ruth Gikow, painted a large oil "Battle at Fort Dix" in 1969 which was exhibited at the Forum Gallery and reproduced in *Gikow: Collected Works.*

Both radio and television broadcast interviews with young men who had spent time in the stockade at Dix, but the coherent story of what caused the riot and the demonstration at Fort Dix in 1969 was never released to the public.

Recently, the *New York Times* ran an "Op-Ed" piece by the prestigious columnist, William Shannon. Mr. Shannon castigated present-day students for their "disdain for history." He blamed this failing on the young people's need for "instant gratification," "addiction to television" and on their unwillingness to spend "the investment of mental effort and of time which a serious book or a *good newspaper* [emphasis added] requires." There is one crucial fact that Mr. Shannon omitted (which accounts for the emergence of underground newspapers) and it is that present-day students cannot find many events which they deem important in the so-called "good newspapers." If this is the case, now, when there is so much more coverage available, how can they have anything but disdain for recorded history?

One thing is certain, the Fort Dix Story, an important story to the young, whose peers were the victims, was not told by the Establishment press.

1.

THE RIOT

Official injustice is the greatest of all violence because that's where it begins. Basically, violence is not the policeman who beats you or the soldier who kills you; they're only the visible agents. It is injustice which is behind the club or gun. Revolutionary violence is too often judged by the image it gives, never by its roots. From where does this violence come? Always from injustice. And the worst is injustice in the name of justice.

> —Costa Gavras, *New York Times Magazine*, March 21, 1971

Fort Dix was the largest military installation in the northeastern United States in 1969, covering fifty-five miles of central New Jersey. Entering Dix you drove through a maze of rectangular uniformity. Identical wide avenues and streets intersected each other at right angles. White frame, two-story barracks, squat cinderblock buildings, patches of flat green fields and clumps of trees repeated themselves ad infinitum. Hundreds of identical helmets, packs, rifles lay in geometric piles in front of occasional buildings. Far off, blocks of men in green uniforms stood at attention, marched, or executed gymnastics in unison. Everything read square, squat and same unless by accident you found yourself in the heart of the maze at the OFF LIMITS stockade.

The stockade was a shock. Rolls of barbed wire ten feet high surrounded the area, a snarl against the man-made rectitude around. Inside the rusty wire no grass or trees. Dirt, gravel and the muddy yellow walls of the barracks was all the stockade prisoners saw day in, day out. The stockade consisted of a collection of World War II wooden barracks, built to accommodate two hundred and fifty men. On June 5, 1969, seven hundred men were living there.

The health facilities were outrageous. One shower and two sinks serviced almost a hundred men in one of the barracks.

The buildings had been condemned twenty years earlier. By 1969 the wood had rotted. Most of the barracks were infested with insects. Erratic winter heating, faulty plumbing, windows that never shut all added to the misery of the overcrowded stockade population. The food was poor and there was not enough to feed the swollen numbers.

Worse than the physical conditions were the harassment, racism and cruelty of many of the guards and of the commandant of the stockade. Very few of the men in the stockade were there for crimes of moral turpitude, rape, stealing money from a buddy or assaulting an enlisted man. Over ninety-five percent, and this was admitted by the officers, were there for being Absent Without Leave. Many of these men needed psychiatric help, drug cures, or medical care, but epileptics and attempted suicides were beaten or put in the straps; men suffering from anemia were fed bread and water, and this relentless bestial treatment enraged not only the men who received it but sickened their friends as well.

These were the conditions in the Fort Dix stockade in 1969. On June 5th of that year a series of increased disciplinary measures and brutal beatings caused a riot of two hundred and fifty prisoners and the torture and court-martial of five young American enlistees. The riot became a *cause célèbre* among the young.

Major Andrew M. Casey had recently been put in charge of the stockade. Major Casey was short, stocky, a regular Army officer, with a close-cropped balding head and bright blue eyes. In a subsequent document of inquiry as to the causes of the riot Major Casey revealed that several weeks before the riot he had taken increased "security measures": "Security measures needed to be improved, needed to be tightened up and we put additional security measures into effect. Number one we restricted the number of prisoners in the compound. We took away the pass system that was in effect, which wasn't working effectively, and we instituted a policy of having prisoner movement in the stockade escorted at all times by cadre. The reason I put this policy into effect was because of the overpopulation, overcrowded conditions . . . We also put into effect the policy of frisk-searching each prisoner prior to letting him return to his individual cell block . . . All of these security measures I took were in line with professional correctional treatment practices that are found in other Army confinement facilities as well as Federal penitentiaries. These were considered by me to be routine in nature, spread out over a gradual period of time and

2

I feel that these measures, although they could have been interpreted by the organizers of the riot as means of harassment —I feel that they were—or I put them into effect as sound security measures."

June 5, 1969, dawned gray and humid at the Fort Dix Post Stockade. Carlos Rodriguez Torres was awakened at 5:00 A.M. as usual, as were all the other prisoners in the stockade, but Carlos woke to the dismal walls of a solitary cell in Disciplinary Segregation. Carlos had landed in "Seg," as the inmates called it, for cutting a stockade prisoner's hair without a barber's license. Carlos was then in his early twenties, a tall, handsome Puerto Rican young man. He had grown up on the Lower East Side of Manhattan and in Puerto Rico. He had enlisted in the Army in 1967 when he was turning eighteen, hoping that the Army would help him kick his heroin habit.

While waiting for his breakfast of dry cereal, bread and water, Carlos sat on his bare metal bunk as he would for the better part of that day and as he had every other day of his sentence in Segregation. It was Carlos' fourteenth day in Disciplinary Segregation. He was forbidden to lie down, to talk or to sing in his solitary cell.

Carlos had slashed his wrists on May 25th. Despite the loss of blood then and his weakened condition, Carlos was kept on a punitive diet described by the Army as "balanced portions of all items in the regular daily ration prepared and served other prisoners *except** meat, fish, poultry, eggs, butter, sweets, desserts, milk and milk products, fruit, fruit and vegetable juices, sugar, salt, pepper, catsup and mustard. Water is the only drink furnished."

In the larger compound when the men finished their breakfast they were ordered to stand in formation for head count. But this morning a new procedure followed. Guards frisked each prisoner. They spread-eagled each man against a wire fence, felt all parts of his body. The soldiers were accustomed to being searched before and after visits with friends and relatives on Sunday or before and after consulting with their lawyers, but not after a meal. This constituted a new indignity and the possibility that they would be subjected to this additional harassment after each meal added one more dismal prospect to the grim days ahead.

At 9:00 A.M. the entire stockade (except the Seg prisoners) massed in the compound. They were ordered to stand at parade

* Emphasis added

3

rest. Each prisoner stood, feet a shoulder-width apart, hands folded behind the small of the back, body rigid, eyes staring straight forward. All prisoners were dressed in fatigues: long-sleeved shirts, long pants bloused in heavy boots and army baseball hats; all clothing buttoned in proper military style. The men stood at rigid attention for three hours. It had grown increasingly hot and humid.

At 12:30 the prisoners from Cell Block 67 marched to lunch; among them was a freckled-faced redhead, Tom Catlow. Tom, the son of a bartender in New Jersey, had been railroaded into the Army at age sixteen. The judge of a juvenile court gave him the choice of three years in the Army or an indefinite five in jail. Tom enlisted.

On their way to lunch Tom and the other inmates saw four guards dragging Jose Ramoz across the compound. Jose had been furious earlier that day when he was ordered to have white-walls (hair shaved around the sides of the head leaving the top regulation length) and he had let the other prisoners know his feelings on the subject. Because of Jose's recalcitrant behavior, Captain Williams, a much disliked black guard, had strapped Jose to a barber chair and shaved his head, giving him not the ordered white-walls but worse, a baldy. When they unstrapped him, Jose Ramoz had smashed everything in sight and pushed his hands through the barbershop windows.

Two years later Tom Catlow remembered the incident vividly: "They had Jose about twenty feet away from us. They started to kick him and beat him. The back of our formation dispersed and we went toward these guys that were beating up Ramoz because everybody knew Jose and dug this guy. When they saw us coming the guards picked Ramoz up. They ran with him to the dispensary and locked themselves in the dispensary. Then the guards taking us to lunch re-formed us and took us to the mess hall. They yelled at us that nobody had given the order to get out of formation and we'd better get back in line or we'd land in Seg with Jose."

At lunchtime the prisoners from Cell Block 67 had to wait a half hour in front of the mess hall. Every man was hot and thirsty from his morning in the sun. When they got inside the men from Cell Block 66 were halfway through their meal. There was nothing to drink because there were no bowls to drink from. James B. Chobot sat facing the dishwasher and plate dryer. He saw bowls being put out for use, and he rose from his chair. A guard told him to sit down. He said he was thirsty and he

4

wanted to get something to drink. The guard said that there was a new rule that once you put your tray down and sat down you were not to rise again until the meal was over. Chobot repeated that he was thirsty and wanted something to drink that in fact all the prisoners were thirsty. An officer said to sit down, that nobody was to get up. Chobot asked why it was wrong to have something to drink and what authority did the guard have to deny the men something to drink. He was told that he had better sit down. Sixty men stood up at the long wooden tables. Sergeant Murray heard the commotion from the orderly room, came in and gave a direct order to sit down. A refusal of a military order can be a matter of an additional five years in the stockade if the authorities want to press charges. All the men sat down. Chobot appealed to the officers on behalf of the men again but in the end sat down and finished his dry meal as did all the other prisoners.

Terry Klug had been sitting directly across from Chobot. Terry was already something of a celebrity. He had helped form RITA (Resistance in the Army) in Europe. A group of enterprising young moviemakers from the Columbia University School of Journalism had made a half-hour film "War Within the Army" covering Terry's flight from Paris, his return to the American Army, his stopover at Kennedy Airport en route to Fort Bragg, his startling apprehension by the military police, and his incarceration in the Fort Dix stockade. In the stockade Terry was one of two whites who chose to bunk upstairs in Cell Block 66 with the black and Puerto Rican prisoners. Terry recalled the Chobot incident at Dix in vivid detail:

"They called in a couple of guards thinking there was going to be trouble. We were all talking about what had happened and we taunted the other prisoners with, 'Hey man, why didn't you stand up, man? See what these pigs are doing to us?' We finished our meal and then as usual we stood in formation. We were still very tense. We marched back to the cell block. When we stood in front of the cell block Sergeant Douglas called Chobot to the orderly room. We knew the order came from the higher-ups in Control, so ten to fifteen of us fell out of rank to go with Chobot. We were told to fall back in rank. We refused. We said that if Chobot was going to the orderly room, we were going too. Chobot had a tremendous amount of respect in the stockade, not as a bully or anything, just as a really good guy. Chobot is white, but the Puerto Ricans, the blacks, everyone really respected Chobot, so when he himself told us to fall back, that he thought he could square things up with these people and that there was no cause to start trouble, we obeyed him. We went inside the cell block which is surrounded by storm fences with a lock. We saw them march Chobot up to Control,* so we knew he would be speaking with Casey or one of the top officers. At that time we didn't dream they would take him down to Seg because that would have been too stupid of them. We thought they just wanted to talk things over and maybe listen to him as our spokesman.

"We were all watching from upstairs in 66 and 67 to see him return when to our shock we saw them march him down to the maximum security area, to Seg. That infuriated just about everyone."

Hardly had Chobot been marched to Seg when a new order was issued to the men. The prisoners in Cell Block 66 were to switch with the prisoners in Cell Block 67. Men who were upstairs in 66 were to move downstairs in 67 and vice versa. No explanation was given, but most of the prisoners assumed, as did Terry Klug, that this was a racist act on the part of the guards so that they could get at the blacks more easily. Many of the blacks were Panthers or Muslims, both frowned on by the Army. They and the Puerto Ricans had chosen to segregate themselves in the top of the cell blocks because they felt that many of the white prisoners were "dime droppers" (informers) and because the guards rarely went upstairs.

Before the prisoners from Cell Blocks 66 and 67 completed the switch of moving their footlockers and bedding they were ordered into another formation. They were to be inspected by Major Casey. The prisoners stood in formation from 1:30 to 5:30 P.M. Major Casey never made his inspection.

While standing rigid at parade rest in the compound the prisoners saw guards searching through their belongings. Shaving cream in a can was contraband, as was any brand of toothpaste but the Army-issue brand. These, when found, were confiscated. Each prisoner was allowed only one pen or pencil. Extras were confiscated. Each prisoner was allowed only ten personal letters. Any additional letters if found were destroyed. Heads started to turn to check on what was happening to personal belongings in front of Cell Block 66. The guards yelled: "Eyes front!"

All eyes were obediently gazing straight across the compound when five guards appeared taking a Puerto Rican prisoner down to Seg. One of the guards pushed him. The prisoner

_____
* Office of the highest-ranking officers.

6

turned around and swung at the guard. Then all the guards attacked the prisoner, threw him down and beat him up. The prisoners in formation started to scream and yell. Other prisoners ran out of their cell blocks and added their cries. The guards dragged the prisoner down to Seg. Twenty guards came down from control and personnel. Major Casey and more guards appeared. Five or ten minutes later an ambulance pulled up at Seg. Hardly had the prisoner been put into the ambulance than another prisoner named Michael Pena was escorted to Seg. Several men in the formation had spent time with Pena in Seg months back when he had slit his throat, been taken to the hospital, had it sewn up and been returned to Seg. One guard was escorting Pena. Michael started to run away from the guard, shouting, "You're not going to put me in Seg! You're not going to beat me any more!" and continued screaming about the beatings he had received. Sergeant Murray came over and talked to him and Pena disappeared into Seg. This all took place before supper.

Supper was cold and there wasn't much of it. Again, there was nothing to drink.

After his "rabbit chow" supper in solitary, Carlos Rodriguez Torres was released from Seg. Major Casey came to the cell to release him. As Carlos remembers it, Major Casey asked him: "Are you ready to go out, Rodriguez?" Carlos answered that yes, he was ready to leave, adding the gratuitous comment that nobody he knew would want to stay there. Casey went on, "You know you've been here quite a few times." And Carlos answered that yes he knew that. Then Major Casey threatened him with, "If you return you're going to be here a long time. Three strikes and you're out." Carlos said that he didn't plan on returning. Within twenty-four hours Carlos would be back, one of thirty-eight men accused of instigating a riot in which two hundred and fifty men participated, though why Carlos was chosen as an instigator when he had been in solitary up until two hours before the riot remains a mystery.

Back in the compound, Carlos had hoped that he would land in a cell block with his friend "Coco," Hector Mayoral (the barber in whose shop Rodriguez had been apprehended) but because of the 66-67 switch he ended up in the wrong cell block. His razor blades and cigarettes were returned to him and he was escorted over to the cell block. As he remembers it, when he got to Cell Block 66: "There was this shammy dude [guard] sitting there. It was hot. He had his fatigue shirt open, just sitting back, like he was on the beach. He had a book open on his leg.

7

Several new guys out from Seg like me gave him their names. He told them to go ahead and find a bunk. He told me, 'Rodriguez, go find your bunk.' I looked for a bunk on the bottom floor. There were none. I saw Frederick Rodriguez (no relation but a friend who'd spent time with me in the dispensary). He went upstairs with me and we couldn't find any empty bunks there either. Finally we found a bed frame against the wall. We talked a little while and I asked where Coco was. He explained about the cell block switch. I went downstairs over to the fence between the cell blocks, asked a prisoner to call Coco over. When Coco came near the fence and saw the bandages on my wrists, he looked at me a long while and asked, 'Why?' I told him not to ask me why. You see I had visited Coco in the hospital when he had cut his wrists because his wife was dying and she hadn't even wanted him to come home to see her. At that time I had told him, 'Man, I don't care what happens, I'll never try to kill myself.' And here I was with the bandages on my wrists. I started to come closer to the fence that divided 66 from 67 when Coco said, 'Get away from the fence. They're busting people for coming near the fence. The brass is really coming down hard now.' He asked me for a pack of cigarettes so I threw him a pack over the fence. I went back to Cell Block 66, showered and shaved, went downstairs and picked up a *Reader's Digest,* skimmed through it, started to smoke a cigarette when I heard this *boom!* The first thing I thought was that there was a fight. I went upstairs and everybody was running around, coming downstairs, throwing footlockers, lights going out, screaming, trying to set fires. I took one look and decided I better get out. Everybody was running downstairs. I went outside to the front gate. I was standing there when Casey came past with these grenades under his arms. He came over to me and he said, 'Rodriguez, I just let you out an hour and a half ago and look what you've done.' I said, 'I had nothing to do with this, sir.' "

When the prisoners from Cell Block 67 returned from supper to their new quarters in Cell Block 66, they were frisked again. Tom Catlow had just been frisked and was on his way into the cell when Doug Sopata, a six-foot-two, blond fellow, threw his field jacket over the fence to Tom. There were Q-tips and shaving lotion in the jacket. Private Chambers caught Tom and Doug in the act, called them outside and threatened them with Seg.

Doug Sopata was liked and trusted by the officers. While

the other men had been standing at parade rest for most of the day, Doug had been working in the records department and had heard a lot of scuttlebutt. He had heard of the 66 and 67 cell block switch before the men, including himself, were given the order. He remembered the evening of the riot vividly:

"We went to supper and there was another incomplete meal. I think I had a cold piece of chicken wing, a very meaty piece of wing, you know how meaty they are, and a couple of pieces of vegetable. It was like they were running out of food. Anyway, after Chambers had caught Tom and me in the jacket incident, I happened to see the guy I worked with in Corrections. I told this guard what had happened about the jacket, and he said not to worry, he'd talk to Private Chambers; so after we straightened things out upstairs Chambers called Tom and me downstairs and addressed me with, 'I know you, you haven't given us any trouble. I'm going to let you go. Forget about this. We'll just keep the material' [shaving lotion and Q-tips]. He pointed to Catlow and said, "Tom, I'm doing this with Sopata. I can't do the same thing with you. I know you. You're an instigator, a troublemaker. You're nothing but trouble and if I ever catch you again, I'll bury you, bury you until you're six feet under.' He said, 'I'll get you no matter what.'. He swore on his mother, a personal-type threat.

"Tempers and nerves were getting on edge. The guards had changed; the old MP company had been sympathetic to the prisoners, the new company was just back from Vietnam. Captain McClendon who I worked with came directly from Vietnam, from the Long Binh stockade. He came to Dix with the Long Binh attitude. He's the one who had just issued the white-wall haircuts. He threatened some men with baldies. About a week before the riot he would just point to people and say, 'Go, take it all off' and they would have to have all their hair shaved off, which was actually illegal by the Army's own code.

"It was about two hours after Private Chambers threatened Tom that the disturbance broke out. I was watching *The Flying Nun* on TV. I remember the ad was on when, *crash!* Then another crash and I thought that something or someone had gone out the window. Then yelling and screaming, 'We want Chobot,' 'It's a riot!' *'Viva la Revolucion!'* I ran back to my bunk, got my bedroll and got my hat. Even if the whole place was burning I'd still go to get my hat. It's a habit. When I got my hat, I ran down with the other guys, Bill Brakefield, Jeff Russell and Steve Comisso. We ran down to the fence. We stood at the fence that divided Cell Block 66 from 65. The guards

9

were there and kept telling us to get back inside. At that time no one wanted to go back inside. For one thing it was dangerous; for another, if they found you inside they'd accuse you of being a rioter.

"The riot squad came with their shotguns, pointing them at us. We all dropped to the ground. When they moved on to 67, we went under and over the fence to 65, at which point they opened the fences and we were herded into the little play area they had over there for us. They told us to sit down and relax, that it was all over. Major Casey came around and yelled to everybody, 'Hope you had fun. You're all going to pay for this. We're going to make an example of you.' Captain McClendon yelled over the loudspeaker, 'Sorry for what I did. No more haircuts.' Anything to quiet the guys down, but it was when Casey yelled, 'Cool it' over the loudspeaker that the fires really got started."

Shortly before the riot on Thursday, June 5, 1969, stockade officials were told by a prisoner informer that a disturbance would take place at approximately 8:00 P.M. They were informed that the prisoners in Cell Blocks 66, 67, 83 and 84 would participate. No motives were established to support this rumor. At approximately 7:45 P.M. Second Lieutenant James Patrick Murray, who was officer of the day in the stockade, advised his guard commanders of this information and further advised the shift leaders and NCOs from A Compound and C Compound, in which the four cells were located. They were to make an immediate check to determine if these cell blocks contained empty footlockers upstairs; if they found any they were to have them moved downstairs where guards could keep them under constant surveillance. At 8:05 P.M. Second Lieutenant Murray was informed by his shift leaders that they had complied with his instructions and had found no evidence to support the rumor about prisoner disturbance.

At 8:10 P.M. Second Lieutenant Murray received a call from the upper Control guard commander in Cell Block 67 that prisoners had begun throwing footlockers out windows. The officer of the day immediately put the alert plan into effect and reserve forces were called up. Major Casey was notified along with other key personnel. While the officer of the day was making a physical check of Cell Block 67, Major Casey, carrying tear gas grenades in each hand, accompanied by several other officers carrying more grenades, went over to Cell Blocks 66 and 67. He then returned to the stockade control room and requested over the stockade public address system that the prisoners return to their cell blocks and quiet down. At this time Second Lieutenant Murray observed another outbreak in Cell Block 84, and reports were received in the control room that fires had started in Cell Blocks 66 and 67. Major Casey then requested that the Alert Force proceed into the stockade.

The fire truck arrived in the stockade at 8:40 P.M. and by 9:30 the fire chief reported that all fires were out and that there were no electrical wires left inside Cell Blocks 66, 67 or 84. The Alert Force of approximately seventy-five men entered the stockade at 9:45 P.M. They surrounded the men who had been herded into the "old Seg" area with shotguns. One guard called out individual names and one by one the prisoners were returned to their cell blocks.

During the riot Sergeant Douglas had told Private Chambers to try to identify the rioters. The sun was setting behind Cell Blocks 66 and 67 at the time of the riot. The lights were out inside the cell blocks, and flames were flickering. Prisoners were rushing in and out to rescue the television set in one cell block, the radio in another, their footlockers and bedding, while other men were throwing footlockers and cigarette butt cans out windows, setting fires, ripping out wires and installations. Some guards and prisoners said it was impossible to identify which men were the rioters.

When the men were released from old Seg and got back to their cell blocks it was dark. They were ordered to clean up the cell blocks outside as well as inside, to pick up all the glass. They couldn't see the glass. Several men were badly cut, Tom Catlow among them. Upstairs and downstairs the floors were flooded, mattresses soaked. Men were lying on their springs. Sergeant Douglas came into Cell Block 66 and told the men to get moving, to get on with the cleaning. Some prisoners started again, others faked. Tom Catlow couldn't get permission to go to the hospital to stop the flow of blood from a deep gash in his foot, so he ripped up a sheet and bandaged it as best he could. The men in 66 and 84 went to sleep at 2:00 A.M. on June 6th. They were awakened at 5:00 A.M. and told that they were now considered maximum security prisoners.

All morning and afternoon of June 6th men from Cell Blocks 66, 67 and 84 were called away in groups of eight or ten to Mental Hygiene or to the Chapel. The remaining prisoners didn't know what was going on. Terry Klug, eager to find out just what this was all about, switched places with one of the men who was last in line of a group of ten to be taken to the Chapel. At the door of the Chapel Terry spotted two plain-clothes CID (Criminal Investigation Division) agents. When it was Terry's turn they asked him his name and cell block; and when he said Terry Klug, Cell Block 67, they said that they'd been waiting for him and that they'd heard his name mentioned over and over. They spoke to him about his articles in *The Bond* (American Servicemen's Union's paper) and other underground military papers. They took him back to the Chaplain's office and proceeded to pull out a whole stack of alleged statements from other prisoners incriminating him. Terry wasn't allowed to read any of the statements or to actually see who had signed them, but one of the agents assured him that they had enough incriminating signed statements to put him away for life. They gave Terry a Salem cigarette and dismissed him into the main Chapel area.

Terry was shaken. The irony of using the Chaplain's office and the Chapel for this purpose suddenly struck him and angered him further. He had just started smoking the cigarette when a friend asked if he could have a drag. They were all hurting for cigarettes and Terry gave him a drag. The friend was sitting at a little table where he had just been interrogated by an agent. He said, "Klug, they told me that if I signed a statement against you that they'd let me out of the stockade for good." Terry realized that the stack of papers he'd been shown in the Chaplain's office might very well be just what the agents had said and not an empty threat. He asked his friend what he'd done. The friend assured Terry that he hadn't signed a statement against him but that he thought Terry ought to know what the CID were up to and undoubtedly some prisoners would sign, being offered an immediate release from the stockade. Terry told his friend to keep the cigarette. He didn't feel like smoking anymore. He felt sick. He walked over to the recreation hall next door.

The great majority of prisoners who had finished being interrogated by the CID were seated there. Some prisoners had been there since early morning without food. When Terry got to the recreation hall there were fifty men sitting around; a great group of them ran over and told him, "Hey man, they're all using your name," "They're all asking your name." Terry asked them in turn whether they had accepted the bribe; whether they had finked on him or anybody else. They all assured him they hadn't. But Terry insisted that someone must have been doing it since the CID had compiled all these signed statements. Terry thought he recognized a few men who might have finked on him because they looked away when he came in. But he felt he understood the pressures they were under and he couldn't get angry at anyone for wanting to find a quick way out of the stockade.

Terry had been in the recreation room for about ten minutes when a Sergeant Smith came from Control, and asked if there was a Terry Klug in the room and if he would please step to the front. Terry stepped to the front and Sergeant Smith said, "Major Casey would like to talk to you in his office." Terry was not taken to Major Casey but to a cage in Control: a room eight feet long and four feet across with a wire mesh locked door. He was left there for several hours and then handcuffed and taken down to the back entrance of Seg. He was the first prisoner to be taken to Seg from the riot suspects. At that time the maximum security area was filled with prisoners on other charges so the guards had to let a prisoner out to make room for Terry. Terry started to write a letter to his lawyer, Rowland Watts of the Workers Defense League, telling him that he thought he was going to be charged with something or other and that he would appreciate Rowland's coming down to Dix as soon as possible. He was writing the letter when a guard came by and told him that he was on DS (Disciplinary Segregation) and that he couldn't have access to writing material or books, so Terry tore the letter up and flushed it down the commode. He gave the guard his pen and notebook.

At first Terry thought that he was going to be the only prisoner accused of the riot, but when they cleared the rest of the fourteen cells out he knew they were making room for more men. All through the night and early into the morning he could hear them being brought in.

Doug Sopata's turn with the CID came toward the end of the evening of June 6th. He was brought into a Mental Hygiene office: "There were two pale, skinny CID agents. One did all the talking:

CID AGENT: Well, Sopata, we got you. We know you're a ringleader.

SOPATA: I might as well keep my mouth shut until I can get myself a lawyer.

CID AGENT: I tell you what, you can get yourself out of it. How much time do you have?

SOPATA: I have two years on a desertion charge.

13

CID AGENT: How'd you like to go home in a few weeks?

SOPATA: Sure, everybody would like to go home in a few weeks.

CID AGENT: I want you to cooperate with us, testify as to what you saw and you'll be home with your wife. [They knew the name of my wife and they knew I had a young daughter.] We have statements against Russell, Catlow and Brakefield; we don't know about Klug. Can you add anything to that?

SOPATA: I don't know anything. I was outside the whole time.

CID AGENT: How could you be outside the whole time when you threw footlockers out the window?

SOPATA: If I had thrown a footlocker out the window it would have been my own. I didn't throw any footlocker out the window.

CID AGENT: I tell you what, sign this piece of paper and we'll have you out of here in a few weeks. [The piece of paper they put in front of me said, "Statement," nothing else on it.] Sign it. We'll fill in the details.

"I thought and thought about it. I could be out in three weeks. I said, 'No, I'm not going to do it.' They had a tape recorder going under the desk. At this point a big black guy came in and said: 'We'll protect you from the men you testify against because they'll all be going into Seg tonight.' I said: 'I saw nothing and I will not sign a blank piece of paper against anybody, especially my fellow man.' He kicked the chair from under me and I walked out. As I was leaving the skinny guy said: 'We'll see you tomorrow. Maybe you'll change your mind after being in the straps.' "

Ten minutes after Sopata got back to the cell block Captain McClendon asked to speak to Tom Catlow and Bill Brakefield. Bill Brakefield, like Terry Klug, was already something of a hero but for very different reasons. Bill was one of the first GIs to take sanctuary on the East Coast. Bill is tall and lanky with a romantically handsome head and tender manner. He was the first soldier to take sanctuary in a university rather than in a church. He was nineteen at the time, and his statement, widely quoted

14

in the press, impressed a host of adults and hundreds of young resisters.

> I want this sanctuary to be completely pacifist. I don't want people calling the police "pigs" or physically confronting them. I don't want anyone hurt.

Though an ardent pacifist, Bill was one of the thirty-eight to be accused of fomenting the riot and one of the five singled out for courts-martial.

As Doug Sopata remembered it: "Bill asked Captain Williams and Captain McClendon whether they would give their word as officers that Tom and Bill would not be taken to Seg. Both officers agreed. Bill turned to the rest of us and said, 'You heard that didn't you?' Everybody said, 'Yes.' They were taken to Control. They told me later that Major Casey and Sergeants Smith and Davidson just laughed when they heard the two had been promised not to be put in Seg. Bill and Tom were handcuffed and taken down to Seg."

Catlow remembered his entry into Seg: "They took us outside, out of Control, out to the sally port. There were thirty MPs with billy clubs. They took us down to Seg the back way. As we walked toward Seg they were carrying out a prisoner who'd had his face bashed in. He'd been put in the straps and dropped. They took him to the hospital.

"They took us in one at a time. I went first. They took my handcuffs off and they searched me. As they searched they took my clothes off and kept kicking my legs out from under me so I kept falling down. When they got me completely stripped they put me in the shower room. Sergeant Whitlow came in, stood me against the wall and pounded me in the chest and yelled, 'Hope you had a lot of fun last night because we had a lot of laughs and we know you did it.' Then they threw me into the cell. They brought the guys in one at a time. You could hear them kick their legs out from under them. You could hear the guys hit the ground. Prisoners started yelling to leave the men alone. Terry screamed 'Let them alone! If you want to hit somebody, come into my cell and hit me!'

"I was in the first cell on the left-hand side if you were facing toward the back and I could see into the shower room. When they brought Jeff Russell in I watched a sergeant knock him up against the wall and smack him across the face while Jeff was handcuffed behind his back. The sergeant said, 'What do you think your father is going to say about this?' After they put Jeff in the cell we heard him screaming: 'Don't kick me! Don't beat me!'

"What really pissed me off was I had just gotten a pipe in the mail. My father had bought me a ten-dollar pipe. They dumped all the stuff from my pockets on the floor. Specialist 4 Humphreys (who was promoted to E5 afterwards) stomped on my pipe and smiled at me. It really bothered me, not because the pipe cost money, but it was the idea that my father went out of his way to send me a pipe and this creep had to stomp on it, just to prove that he had some kind of balls.

"During the night, every half hour, the guards that were on came through and kicked the cells, woke us up and told us to get up. We had to sleep on the bare bunks in our clothes, no mattresses or anything. The next morning we asked when we were going to get mattresses, pillows and bedding, the guards told us to shut up. We couldn't talk. We were put on Code 13, D.S. For three days we weren't allowed to shower and shave, to get our fifteen minutes of exercise. We kept asking for 5-10s, the form you fill out to get a lawyer, counseling, mental hygiene, a doctor, anything at all. You're supposed to get a 5-10 whenever you want.

"One day I was taken with shackles on my legs and handcuffs to the CID. The agent who interviewed me told me I was going to get about three hundred and fifty years, that I was charged with mutiny and conspiracy to mutiny, riot, aggravated arson, destruction of government property and a few other things. He told me that if I would sign a statement against Brakefield, Russell, Rodriguez and Klug, they wouldn't charge me for the riot, that I'd get out of the stockade, and out of the Army. When they threaten you with a few hundred years you get scared. The CID agent said that many people had ratted on me and that I should rat on some people. I cried. I was very frightened. He told me that if I signed the paper I wouldn't get into any trouble. I signed it. As I walked out my face was all red and I was crying. The other agent came over and patted me on the back. They gave me some real food to eat and took me back to the stockade and into the cell and I stayed there.

"Every day for months we went through this total harassment, sixteen hours a day (because you slept eight of them), guards yelling at you every time you opened your mouth. Just screaming and yelling at you to shut up or to tell you you weren't sitting properly. The first three or four weeks that we were down there, all the mail we wrote was handed back to us with 'Contains information on the riot.' The contents of mine

16

was: 'Dear Mom, I am being charged with mutiny, conspiracy, arson, riot and many other things. Could you get me a lawyer? I'm in trouble. I need some help.' I was told that I couldn't tell my parents what I was being charged with or anything concerning the riot. Right after I was told that, the Chaplain came down and asked me if it was all right for him to write my parents. I said: 'Fine only there's just one thing; it's not going to sound too good if you write to them and I don't. They're going to think something's wrong. The Army hasn't proved that I've done anything wrong yet but if I don't write my parents and tell them and you do, my parents will think I caused the riot.' The Chaplain said there was nothing he could do about that.

"Finally our letters started to get out. You were never sure of what really got mailed and what didn't. All our mail for the next months was censored. All our mail went to Major Casey. He read everything we wrote.

"After the ninth week we started to get 5-10s. I put in a good twenty-five 5-10s to Captain Monte who had defended me at my escape trial. It was another three weeks before I saw him. He had only received two 5-10s out of all the ones I'd made out. He explained that he wouldn't be able to defend me."

Andrew Stapp of the American Servicemen's Union believes that the officers deliberately caused the June 5th riot sensing that the men were becoming increasingly discontented, that something was brewing, and hoping to bring trouble to a head before the uprising was too big to handle. Many of the prisoners believe that the weeks of increasing harassment, the series of guards' brutalities, irrational commands and the unreasonable treatment of Chobot on June 5th caused them and their fellow prisoners on their own into the feral burst of destructive action. Whatever the causes, it is utterly clear that the prisoners wanted to bring to the attention of a larger American public the treatment they were suffering as Americans by Americans on American soil.

A stockade riot is a very desperate measure on the part of prisoners. All the prisoners mentioned in this chapter ended up in Disciplinary Segregation, in solitary cells 8 x 6 x 4. They lost between fifty and sixty pounds each on "rabbit chow." They had not yet been found guilty or innocent but awaited their trials for months caged like animals and treated in ways that would not be approved of by the ASPCA.

The Army announced to the public that thirty-eight men

had been brought up on charges stemming from the riot. Some of these men were given special courts-martial and dismissed. Others received acquittals due to lack of evidence. Charges were dropped for a number of others. Among those whose charges were dropped was Tom Tuck, accused of being a Black Panther. He was dragged from his cell and thrown into Segregation with nineteen other men still awaiting trial on charges pending from the riot. He spent two months in Seg before the riot charges were dropped against him. He was then court-martialed for being AWOL and given the maximum sentence of six months, despite the fact that he had already spent three and a half months in pre-trial confinement.

From the original thirty-eight charged, five men were singled out for general courts-martial facing maximum sentences of fifty years each. Their trials deserve a considered review by each tax-paying citizen.

2.

THE COFFEEHOUSE AND *SHAKEDOWN*

Military injustice in America, on North American soil, is most palpable in the stockades and brigs that darken this country. But a system of injustice and cruelty cannot be kept within barbed wires. It spreads. Young civilians who have created coffeehouses and newspapers near military bases all over North America have suffered the relentless ruthless tactics of the military, often in collusion with State Police and right-wing groups. Hardly a coffeehouse remains standing; they have been bombed, razed, raided or their staffs have been illegally dispossessed and jailed. The Fort Dix Coffeehouse, the fourth to be formed in North America, is no exception. It started as the others as an outgrowth of the peace movement, by a group of young people opposed to the war in Vietnam, young people opposed to drugs and violence.

Less than a year before the stockade riot in Fort Dix, close to election time of 1968, the Student Mobilization group initiated a GI Week. One of the activities planned for this week was a picnic at Fort Dix. On November 2nd several busloads of students left New York City and headed for Wrightstown, New Jersey.

On arriving in Wrightstown, the group walked to Fort Dix and gathered on a grassy area just outside the base proper. Either because of the inclement weather—it was a raw, wet day —or because the GIs had been warned not to fraternize with this group, which in fact they had been, not many GIs joined the picnic; so the picnickers left that area and sludged back to Wrightstown where they visited every last diner and restaurant and talked with the GIs there.

For many of these students this was their first visit to a military base, their first conception of working politically with GIs. These concerned young people were tired and discouraged from working with other students just like themselves, getting nowhere; tired of seeing their political energies turned into a destructive divisiveness which was ultimately to end in a split with the Weatherman faction, dedicated to destructive tactics per se. One concrete disagreement they had with this radical segment was that the latter considered all GIs "pigs," whereas these young people felt that GIs were people like themselves and deserved to be educated and helped.

A small enthusiastic group grew out of the November 2nd excursion. They met often and held long exploratory talks. The upshot of these talks was the decision to open up a coffeehouse near Dix. From the beginning they met with foul play. Beth Reisen, a soft-spoken, compassionate student, who had left Radcliffe after her sophomore year, recalled the hard-nosed resistance the early search for a coffeehouse engendered:

"We started right away looking for a place to open up. We found one quite quickly, end of November or early December. We went in with a lawyer, talked to the landlord's agent, drew up a lease. The agent said, 'Fine, everything's ready to go but I advise you, don't sign the lease until you get a business license from the city council for your own protection.' This was in Wrightstown. We applied to the city council for a business license. The small business license was applied for by one of our members, an affluent young Princeton graduate with very good credentials. The city council meets once a month and normally it takes one month to get such a license. They gave us the runaround. By the end of the second month the board was telling us that they were holding back on the license because they hadn't received the report on our Princeton graduate from Chicago. Now Chicago was where he was born, but he hadn't lived there since he was three years old—of which they were perfectly well aware. While we were waiting and not getting the license we went back to the landlord's agent to sign the final papers on the lease, at which point he suddenly said no, with no explanaiton. The irony is that at the end of three months we got our license. This landlord was a very big landlord. He owned two blocks of Wrightstown, also cemeteries and shopping centers in Florida."

While the coffeehouse was in the throes of becoming a reality, a young college graduate, Sam Karp, had decided to join the Army to try to organize within the Army.

". . . I conceived the idea with several friends from the New England Resistance of going into the military and organizing GIs. One was a 4F, one a 1Y and I was 1A. I'd gone through four years of ROTC at college. Just before I graduated I refused my commission. The commanding officer told me I couldn't. Like most military matters, the military didn't know their own laws. I read the regulations and found that I could simply refuse the commission to become an officer and that they would have to give me time to find a reserve unit.

"Before I made a final decision I came to New York and met with Rennie Davis for the first time. This was in the fall of 1968. Rennie was working on an anti-election campaign and was setting up a 'Support Our GIs Week' at Fort Dix. I told Rennie that if I went into the Army from Boston I would more than likely be sent to Fort Dix. Then I went to talk to Andy Stapp who was new to me too. We talked at length about his experience at Fort Sill and the ideas that he had about organizing the Army. From New York I went to Philadelphia where I met with some old friends in the resistance and told them that I might be in Fort Dix and that I was beginning to think about putting out a newspaper when I got there. They thought it was a good idea and said to keep in touch. Then I returned to Boston where I joined a reserve unit. I figured that if I enlisted, or allowed myself to be drafted I would face the possibility of going to Vietnam. At that point I knew I wouldn't go and couldn't see how I would start any kind of resistance if I were in a stockade for several years. I had no intention of applying for a CO because I'm not a pacifist. So I joined the reserve unit. In November of 1968 I was called to active duty for what was supposed to be six months of basic training at Fort Dix.

"I went in with my hair pretty long and a moustache. They shave your head. We used to hang towels over the mirrors in the morning. You didn't want to see how you looked. You kept looking at other people, wondering if you looked that bad. Most of the kids that come into Basic suffer a real culture shock. No separate stalls for toilets. People having to shit next to somebody makes a lot of them really uptight. It's a culture shock, the communal living, and then many of them have problems, leaving girlfriends, wives, not wanting to leave their families, not wanting to go into the Army, afraid about Vietnam which is on *everybody's* mind from the first day they get there.

"Since I was in the reserve, I knew what my orders would be [Clerk-Typist School at Dix] but nobody else knew and they worried that they were going to be sent to Fort Polk for infantry training; from there they knew the next step was Vietnam. So that was always on their minds. I had started talking to guys in my company, making friends and before I knew it, I was made a squad leader. I was called in by the Sergeant.

" 'Karp,' he said: 'You're to have a single room. Everybody else is going to be living in these seven- or eight-man rooms, but you're to have a single room. We've looked at your record and found out that you're a college graduate and we want you to lead these men. You'll have more privileges. You'll have passes every weekend.'

"Immediately what they had done was to set me apart from the others. Whenever the Army senses a troublemaker, they try to set everybody else against that person. I wasn't sure whether that was what was up or not, but after all I had been pretty open in Boston about saying that I was going into the Army to organize.

"I was responsible for a squad. After about a week I had talked to all the guys in the squad: 'Listen, I'm no better than anybody else. They're trying to make me special, but we've all got to get through this together, so we've got to work together.' We built the beginning of a socialist structure inside my squad and the guys really dug it. When we had to clean up, we all cleaned up together. So I was made platoon leader because I was doing such a good job.

"My sergeant was the only person at Fort Dix who had received a Congressional Medal of Honor in Vietnam. He'd been in the Army for twenty years and he'd been busted about twenty times. At that point he was just an E5 with three stripes. He used to get drunk all the time. I learned a lot about what the Army does to people and about lifers from talking to this guy. He knew my views, that I was talking out against the war. He would come to me and say: 'I read Schlesinger's book, *The Bitter Heritage,* and I really think what he was saying was right.' This from a guy who had been to Vietnam three times. I hadn't read the Schlesinger book. He gave it to me and I read it. When I talked to the guys, the Sergeant never let on. He yelled at the guys, training as usual. He felt that most of these guys were going to Vietnam and that it was his job to train them. Otherwise, if he didn't train them, they'd be killed. He felt this responsibility, but there were tremendous contradictions in what he felt about Vietnam and therefore in what he felt about his job. He'd been divorced. His family affairs were really fucked up. He was one confused guy, but I loved him.

"We'd have what they called orientations, where we saw films like *Why Vietnam?* in which President Johnson came on and said: 'Why Vietnam?' This was shown in an auditorium that held about one thousand people. The movie presented the domino theory, that our government pushed at that time. Remember this was 1968. People slept through the movie and then when Johnson came on, people hissed. I was amazed. I felt this consciousness in the auditorium that everybody knew this was bullshit propaganda.

"After the film, a second lieutenant got up and said: 'Those of you who were laughing and hissing and sleeping don't understand that we're fighting in Vietnam to keep our neighborhoods safe at home. Now who wants to say something to that?' Out of a thousand people I found myself raising my hand. He said: 'Yes?' I stood up and did this fifteen-minute riff about why I thought the war was wrong.

"As soon as I had finished, other people started raising their hands and asking questions and we had this great discussion for about two hours. The lieutenant was totally lost. People were laughing at him, saying things like 'I don't think the domino theory is right. I think the Vietnamese people have a right to run their own country and we shouldn't be there.' The officer came back with: 'Well, communism is bad,' and gave a whole red-baiting spiel. People understood it was empty rhetoric, the United States' rhetoric which is as tiresome as the Movement's rhetoric, as any rhetoric.

"One time the Chaplain came to my company of eighty guys. The Chaplain addressed us all solemnly: 'Men, there's something in the Army that you have to learn. It's something I've learned all my life: respect. When I was a boy and my father told me to do something, although I might not agree, I did it because he was my father and I respected him. When I went to college, young men, there were certain rules and regulations at my university that I didn't like, that I didn't want to comply with, but those were the rules and I made the best of it. Men, that's just the way it is in the Army. There'll be certain things that you don't think are right, that you might want to question, but you've got to obey them because they're orders.'

I sat there trying to figure out what I was going to say because I had to answer that one. While I was thinking this innocent kid in my company, a very religious boy, stood up to the Father. 'You know, Father,' he said: 'I think what you're saying is all wrong. If what you are saying was right, we'd all still be Jews.' That broke the ice and everybody was saying: 'I think we have a right to question. . . .' A kid that was gung-ho even got up and said: 'If I'm going to be leading men and I'm responsible for their lives, I should have a right to question what's going to happen to these people.' When I finally was going to put my two bits in, I saw the Company Commander in the back trying to cut the whole thing off, signaling the Chaplain, so the Chaplain said: 'Well men, it's been good talking to you. I'll be in my office any time. My hours are two to five in the afternoon on Thursdays.' When he left, we just laughed. The whole company broke out in laughter. Nobody respects chaplains anymore.

"I started getting literature at Dix. Andy was sending me the *Bond*. I got the resistance paper *The Rat* from New York and *The Militant*. I had issues of these papers in my room all the time. I still had this single room and guys would come in and read the papers if they felt like it. There's a regulation in the Army that you can't distribute literature that might be subversive, but if you don't distribute it, if it's just there, guys can read it, there's no regulation covering that.

"One Sunday I was sitting in my room with two other GIs. We were talking. Some of the newspapers were lying out on my bed and the First Sergeant of the Company, not the Sergeant I was friendly with, but First Sergeant Topp, a big fat sergeant, stormed into my room with a Pfc, one of the cadre in the company.

TOPP: Karp, I understand that you have antiwar literature here.

KARP: Yes, I do, sir.

TOPP: Is that one of them?

KARP: Yes, that's one.

TOPP: Can I see it?

KARP: Sure.

[He picked it up. I think it was *The Militant* . He started to read it.]

TOPP: Karp, I want all of these. Gather 'em up.

[A whole crowd had gathered around my door and I realized that this was going to be my first confrontation. Thanks to my talks with Andy Stapp and Rennie Davis, I knew all the right things to say.]

KARP: Sergeant, you can't have them, sir.

TOPP: Karp, gather them all up. I'm taking them.

[I stood up.]

KARP: No, sir, if you're familiar with AR135-81, a soldier

24

has the right to read and retain any kind of publication. That's what these are and you have no
right to take them, sir.

[He started jumping. He was nervous and shaking. He
could hardly talk; he stuttered.]

TOPP: Karp, I'm going to call the MPs.

"He stormed out of the room. Meanwhile, I'm scared shit-
less. I figured here I go into the stockade. I started explaining
to the guys what had happened. I explained the regulation but
added that regulations don't mean shit. All these guys that had
been gathering outside my room came in and started reading
the papers; then I repeated that they should all know what the
regulation was about having papers but that the only way they
could keep the papers and read them was by just refusing to
give them up. The MPs never came. I kept talking to the guys
and soon we were having informal meetings on Sunday with
about forty guys from my platoon. We'd sit around and talk
about the war. I was getting the *New York Times* sent to me.
Sometimes we would sneak out and buy other papers at the PX.
"That initial confrontation had taken place in the first week
in December. We got two weeks off for Christmas. I went to
Boston to see my old friends there and discuss with them some
of the things I had been doing. Through them I heard that there
were some people in New York who were talking about setting
up a coffeehouse at Fort Dix. The names I was given were
Beth Reisen, Corinna Fales and Bob Tomashefsky. They gave
me Bob's number. I called him and told him that I'd be in New
York before returning to Dix and that I wanted to talk with them.
"When I met Bob, Beth and Corinna at Bob's apartment on
111th Street, there I was, this shaved head, this GI from Fort
Dix. They didn't know any more about me than that, that I was
a GI from Fort Dix who wanted to start a newspaper. All I knew
about them was that they were some Movement people from
New York who wanted to start a coffeehouse. When we started
talking, it was a total turn-on for all of us. I was turned on by
the fact that they were doing something positive in relation to
Dix. They were turned on by the fact that I was a contact at
Dix. We talked about the coffeehouse and they said that though
they were determined to start one, they were not sure how
receptive the GIs would be at Fort Dix. So I offered to get them
together with some of my Sunday group. We would meet in

25

the PX and all sit around and talk. Through January and into February they would come down on Sundays and rap with the guys.

"They started putting out leaflets saying 'Coffeehouse is Coming to Fort Dix' and something to the effect: 'We're civilians from New York who want to support the GI movement and the coffeehouses throughout the country.' They would pass them out, about a thousand every Sunday afternoon, at the Port Authority. Guys in my own company would come back with the leaflets. I told them that I knew these people and that their coffeehouse project seemed like a good idea.

"After the newspapers incident while still in Basic, the Army had me pegged as a troublemaker so they sent me on extra details like KP. They couldn't give me KP in my own company because there was a schedule they had to follow, so they'd send me to other companies. It was great because I got to meet new guys in different companies that normally I wouldn't have had a chance to meet. I began meeting guys who were sympathetic who knew other guys who were thinking along our lines and we started to set up a network all over the base.

"The day we were to graduate from Basic was a big occasion. Five battalions were to graduate and the Commander General was coming down to give a speech. Some of my company decided to put on a demonstration at Fort Dix. We spread the word around. I got in touch with Beth, Corinna and Bob. Several carloads of people came down from New York for the graduation ceremony.

"The plan was that at the end of the General's speech, he'd praised us for training to be fighting men, we would all stand up and give the peace sign. We had spread the word through the five companies. The people from New York who would be sitting with the parents and families would start a peace chant.

"When we marched into the auditorium in formation we were surprised to see the place surrounded by MPs and Federal marshals. When we got in and sat down, we realized that there were CID people in suits. We got the message and decided not to put on any demonstration. Right after the service was over, when the parents and families were mingling with the GIs, our New York contingent came over and started hugging me. They stood out from the other civilians because of their frizzy hair and clothes. Just as they were embracing me, two CID men grabbed me and said: 'Come with us.'

"This was my first encounter with the CID. They took me into a small room and asked me what I had planned for that day and asked if I realized that there were Federal marshals there. They claimed that they didn't know me or what I was up to but had singled me out because of the New York contingent who had come to congratulate me. They went on to threaten me with: 'We had Federal marshals here. We were going to arrest everybody. Do you realize the severity of what you planned to do?' I never agreed that I had planned to do anything and that's the last I heard of it.

"The end of January or beginning of February I was finished with Basic and I was sent to Clerk-Typist School, also at Fort Dix. I had a lot of free time. The first day at Clerk School the Sergeant asked how many of us knew how to type. Four or five of us raised our hands out of a class of twenty. 'Okay, you four or five,' he motioned us, 'you sit over here and practice while the others learn how to type.' I had four weeks of freedom to type articles, write letters.

"Most of the contacts I had made in Basic Training were shipped out but one guy, Ron Krupp, stayed. I had met him the first day of Basic. He was in a company right next to mine. Ron and I came to be close friends. He and I actually started *Shakedown.*

"Ron had filed for a Conscientious Objector as soon as he got into Basic. He refused to train with a gun. After Basic was finished, he was put in this Hold Company waiting for word to come down from Washington about whether they would grant him his CO rating or not. They didn't do much and so he and I had a lot of free time. We walked around the base and met guys in different companies. Ron and I started to pull together a group of people who would work on the paper.

"Whenever I got off on a weekend, I'd go to New York and talk with Bob and Beth about ideas for the paper and the coffeehouse. They kept coming to Wrightstown and distributing their leaflets on the main street.

"The first week in March we started writing *Shakedown.* Ron and I and several friends worked at the Liberation News Service. They let us use their equipment to lay out the paper. We had no money at that point so we started raising money. I raised some money through old resistance friends of mine in Philadelphia and Boston. They gave us enough money to put out the first issue. The rest of the money was raised by the New York group.

"The first issue of *Shakedown* came out on the 23rd of

March, 1969. We distributed it in Wrightstown, and the Port Authority in New York. A group of students from Princeton went to Newark and distributed the paper there. Philadelphia friends of ours distributed the paper at the Philadelphia airport, bus station and train station. I think we printed seven thousand copies. Every single one was gone in two weeks.

"Two days after the paper was out, Gene Packer, who was a co-worker, and I were called in by our company Commander, Colonel Lee, a black Colonel. He started laying out all these regulations, threatening us with being accused of subversion, lowering the morale of the troops, I forget all the specifics but he kept threatening us and threatening us. The First Sergeant of the battalion was standing there throughout the harangue. He looked like Mr. Clean, bald headed, big, he stood there with his arms folded across his chest. It was a very intimidating atmosphere. Gene was scared because this was his first confrontation with the law. Finally I said: 'Listen, I know all the regulations and I can repeat them verbatim. Unless you're going to charge us with something specific, we've got things to do, sir.' He was stunned and speechless and we left.

"Four days later I was released from active duty and sent back to my reserve unit. I still had a month more of training to go through but orders came from the First Army that I should be released to my reserve unit which at that time was in Boston. I decided I was going to stay at Fort Dix and help with the coffeehouse and continue the paper. This was the first week in April. I went home to visit my parents for a week. The second week in April when I came back, Beth and Bob were still having great trouble finding a place for the coffeehouse. So I spent three days on the phone in Wrightstown.

"Wrightstown is a town like most other military towns, filled with hock shops and shyster jewelry stores, hoagie stores and bars and cleaners. The only people that really live in the town, the residents, are mostly dependents of people on the base, or retired Army people or just people that are there to rip off GIs like these loan sharks."

Toward the end of April Sam Karp, Beth Reisen, Bob Tomashefsky and Corinna Fales located a Carvel stand just outside the city limits of Wrightstown which they could rent for $250.00 a month. They couldn't get a permanent lease but by then they were willing to settle for a month-by-month agreement. Their new landlord, Michael Schen, owned and ran an auto shop behind the Carvel stand. Mike had run the ice cream stand for a couple of years but it had been a failure. He had rented the building to a car rental outfit but they left. Michael Schen is a Yugoslav and had been a political prisoner in Yugoslavia. He was very anti-Communist and would tell the coffeehouse workers repeatedly: "We're much freer over here. You should see how they live over there." But from the moment the coffeehouse opened Mike began to get harassed.

First the insurance on the building was cancelled. Very shortly thereafter the windows of the coffeehouse were broken. Mike's wife started to get threatening calls at night which frightened her badly; threats to the effect that she and Mike better get rid of the coffeehouse people or else . . . Children in school started calling the six- and nine-year-old Schen children "Communists."

Formerly the State Police would refer tow-jobs to Mike's shop. This constituted a fairly important part of his income. With the opening of the coffeehouse the police abruptly stopped this practice. They made new regulations. They issued tickets when Mike parked his cars across the street from his shop which they had always permitted before. People down the street at the Gulf station who had let Mike park cars in their empty lot suddenly refused. To top things off the town council told Mike that he had to build an eight-foot fence around his entire property as part of Lady Bird's Highway Beautification Program. But it was the threatening calls to his wife that really got Mike down; still, he needed the $250.00.

The Fort Dix Coffeehouse opened officially on April 23, 1969. The second issue of *Shakedown* ran headlines: THE COFFEE-HOUSE OPENS.

Inside they had painted the walls yellow and red. GIs had brought in posters of revolutionary heroes and pasted them up. One black officer from McGuire Airbase contributed a poster. GIs drew cartoons and posted them. A group of GIs contributed a record player. After payday they would always bring in food for The Coffeehouse. The U.S. Servicemen's Fund contributed underground newspapers from all over the country.

The doors opened around 5:00 P.M. and closed around midnight. It was flexible. At first they served sandwiches, homemade cakes and cookies, coffee and soda. Gradually they stopped serving food until at the end they were only serving coffee and store-bought cookies.

At around 5:00 they would start playing records and the GIs would start coming in. Most nights the GIs would just sit around the small tables talking to the civilians. Anyone interested could join a group in a side room working on *Shakedown.* Some people wrote articles. Others liked to work on layout and the group of about twenty or so decided what ran or didn't. There was never one editor.

Beth Reisen estimated that there must have been thousands who came into The Coffeehouse at least once. She thinks about one hundred men were really changed by their association with The Coffeehouse, either by getting active in Movement work after getting out of the Army, or by starting a paper on a new base if they were transferred, or in more subtle ways:

"We helped lay seeds in a lot of guys so that later when they have to make a decision, if there's a strike in a factory by black guys where they work, they'll come down on the right side.

"Wednesdays and Sundays we'd usually show Newsreel films. Newsreel is a group who make political films, films of demonstrations, films about Wilmington, Delaware, and how the corporation controls it. Newsreel was started by a couple of guys who were close to SDS in the early days, seven or eight years ago.* We had very spirited debates after the movies. One movie we showed, *No Vietnamese Ever Called Me Nigger,* told the story of three black GIs who had been in Vietnam and how they felt when they got back. The discussion after that movie was led by black guys and I think the white GIs learned a lot that night. If we advertised we might get a big audience. Our biggest night was the night the Pageant Players came down. We had over a hundred that night. It was during the summer and we held it outside. We didn't have that kind of room inside. Normally a movie might bring about 75. Some nights it could get very low, particularly on long weekends. We learned to close down on long weekends. On an average night we'd draw about thirty or forty men.

"In the beginning, white GIs' attitudes were essentially, 'If the black guy is picking up shit, I'm usually there wrapping it.' All our talk about the blacks' oppression left them cold. When we spoke about the percentage of blacks in the Army, the percent of black casualties, the percentage of blacks sent to the front lines, it was just our statistics to them. But when the blacks started coming in, then the discussions got heated and in the end there was education and understanding.

"We had blacks coming into The Coffeehouse, which was different from other coffehouses. Most of the black guys on base

* Beth was taped in 1970.

were political on some level and we had a few officers who were sympathetic with us. One black officer who came in almost from the beginning was from McGuire Air Force Base. He had started to organize blacks at McGuire around the issue of allowing black women to be invited to the Service Club dances. At that time they were excluded. In the end this ruling was changed but our friend got a demotion and a lot of harassment. We had quite a few regulars from McGuire.

"The Coffeehouse got to be a nice place where guys could come in and talk and feel open. The official attitude of the Army was to ignore The Coffeehouse but in fact we know that particularly in basic training companies GIs were warned that if they came to The Coffeehouse, they'd get an article fifteen. This was strictly untrue by their own regulations. Fort Dix is mostly a training base and the trainees don't know the rules, so to a certain extent such threats worked, but then sometimes they backfired. We had guys come in and say that they'd never heard of The Coffeehouse but when their drill sergeants told them they'd better not go to this coffeehouse, they decided to come down and see what it was all about.

"Even before we had The Coffeehouse, the Newark ACLU started negotiations with the base to allow *Shakedown* to be distributed. The Army regulation reads: No printed material may be distributed on base without approval of the commanding officer of the base. We wrote and asked for permission to distribute *Shakedown.* They wrote us back and tried to get information out of us as to who published it, edited it, where did the money come from. We didn't answer their queries but asked again if we could have permission to distribute our paper. They wrote back a firm no. This was in April, 1969. Finally it came down to the entire Army that newspapers might receive permission to be distributed on base by the Commander of the base on an issue-by-issue basis. Immediately General Collins, the Fort Dix Commanding General, gave out the statement that *Shakedown* was banned from Fort Dix. Many GIs who had copies of *Shakedown* in their possession got scared and in fact many drill sergeants were confused. No printed material can be banned from a base; the ban is on distribution on base. *Shakedown* could be legally picked up in the The Coffeehouse, or at bus stations, etcetera, or in the mail.

"Before any clear directives had been handed down, Saul Shapiro and Joe LeBanc were distributing *Shakedown* on the base. They had a whole pile of *Shakedowns* in the car. There was a guy sitting by the side of the road, under a tree, who had just slit his wrists. An MP was sitting there with him. The MP caught sight of Joe and Saul, left the guy sitting there bleeding and hauled Joe and Saul to the PMO [Provost Marshal's Office]."

Throughout the history of The Coffeehouse there was continual harassment and threats to the people who worked there. The young civilians who worked there were well aware that by the very nature of The Coffeehouse they were a threat to the military and though the official attitude was to ignore their existence, it was not going to be easy. On the one hand, they had to defend The Coffeehouse, and on the other, they knew that if fights broke out within The Coffeehouse, the State Police, who were right across the street, would close it down; the Army would declare it off base and say that it was a disorderly house.

Suspicious things happened from the very beginning. Screens would be cut. The front door which had been locked the night before would be unlocked in the morning and then the pressure began to build. One late afternoon, Hal Muskat, a GI in a Replacement Company, and Sam Karp were distributing *Shakedown* in Wrightstown when a car pulled up and two GIs jumped out and attacked Hal and Sam. They had a scuffle and Hal ended with a bloody nose. Sam and Hal returned to the coffeehouse. Twenty minutes later, a group of six GIs led by the GI that had jumped them came in. The GI, a huge fellow about six-feet-four and two hundred and forty pounds, marched in and started overturning the tables. He came over to Sam and punched him in the jaw, calling him a Communist. Sam's first reaction was to hit him back, but Josie Biddle Duke (an early Coffeehouse supporter) grabbed his arm. The GI went over and hit Bob a couple of times and Bob just tried to hold him off. The other GIs were overturning tables. There were about twenty regular Coffeehouse GIs and civilians but they understood that they shouldn't get into a free-for-all. The big GI was doing all the talking and pushing around. One of his cohorts was a Puerto Rican boy who just kept looking around at the posters on the walls. Somebody said the police were coming. They heard sirens. The Coffeehouse people had the big GI figured for a CID agent or a right-wing organizer; his followers didn't seem ready to take action. As the sirens came closer, the big GI started backing toward the door, at which point a black GI walked over and said: "Motherfucker, why don't you try and hit me?" The black GI held his hand on his back right pocket. Everybody in The Coffeehouse was sure

32

that he had a razor in it. The white GI just stared. The black GI said, "Go ahead, motherfucker, why don't you hit me?" The white GI started to move and the black GI pulled his knife out of his pocket and cut the guy. His friends carried him away. The State Police came and asked what had happened, as if they knew beforehand something was supposed to happen. The Coffeehouse people said nothing at all had happened.

From the moment The Coffeehouse started, the State Police were always taking pictures of the civilians who were connected with it, writing down their license plates. One day when Bob and Sam were driving down to Dix, on the highway between the turnpike and Fort Dix, they got stopped by a State Policeman. Hardly had they pulled over when another State Police car bore down on them. The policeman accused them of speeding. They knew they hadn't been speeding because they were always extremely careful not to be caught on any misdemeanor. They denied the speeding charge. Asked to produce driver's license and owner's card, Sam was horrified to discover that he had given his to Herb Dreyer the day before and Herb had not returned it. The policeman arrested Sam for speeding and for not having a driver's license. He intimated that since he had a Pennsylvania license plate, the car might very well be stolen. Just before taking him off, the policeman turned to both of them and said: "You're the people who are running that coffeehouse." Sam said: "What coffeehouse?" The State Trooper said: "We know you're the people behind The Coffeehouse." So Sam was taken into Southfield Township to the Justice of the Peace who turned out to be a woman. Sam heard the trooper whisper to the woman: "I want high bail." The woman set $100 bail. Sam didn't have $100 with him and thought it exorbitant for a speeding charge. He called Emerson Darnell, an attorney, who was out, but his partner talked to the trooper. He told the trooper he was going to call the judge to have the bail reduced and to please keep Sam there. The trooper said: "Okay, I'll wait for your call," but as soon as he hung up, he took Sam to the State Police barracks where they tried to interrogate him. He wouldn't talk. Finally word got through that the bail was to be reduced to the $25 Sam had with him. The trooper took him back to the woman justice of the peace's house, way out in the woods somewhere, and he bailed himself out. The trooper refused to drive him back to his car, or back into town. It was a right-wing area, but Sam managed to hitch a ride in a truck back into town where he tried to find Bob.

About ten minutes after they had taken Sam away, Bob was still sitting in the car, hoping they would bring Sam back before too long, when two State Police cars showed up with a tow truck and said they were impounding the car.

BOB: I'll drive it with you to the pound.

1ST TROOPER: No.

BOB: Let me drive it; I have the keys.

1ST TROOPER: No, you ride in the tow truck. [So they towed the car to a garage and demanded the keys to the car. Bob asked for a receipt for the keys. He was refused by the owner of the garage. The State Policeman then asked for his identification card. Bob showed it to him.] Get off this man's private property.

[It was right on the highway. So Bob started walking down the highway with Sam's briefcase under his arm. He had hardly walked a city block when the same police car pulled up and cut him off. This time the two troopers were in it. The trooper who had originally asked to see Bob's ID card asked for it again.]

BOB: You just saw it.

1ST TROOPER: Let's see it again. [No sooner did he get it than he gave it to the second officer, who pocketed it.] Let's see your ID card.

BOB: I just gave it to you.

1ST TROOPER: (yelling): Are you calling me a fucking liar?

BOB: No. I just gave you my ID card.

1ST TROOPER: You're under arrest.

[They charged him with using loud and profane language and being in the state for an illegal purpose.]

When they brought him to the State Police Barracks, they must have been taking Sam out the back door. They took Sam's briefcase from Bob. It had all the mailing lists from GIs who had written in asking for *Shakedown,* a lot of Sam's personal papers and his personal address book. None of these were ever recovered.

34

There was a tiresome series of such incidents so that The Coffeehouse workers spent much of their time and energy bailing each other out of jail. Finally they got so fed up with the whole business that they brought suit against the State Police and the U.S. Army. Sam, Bob and Harold Muskat, a dedicated Coffeehouse worker then a Specialist 4th Class assigned to A Company Special Troops at Fort Dix, and Harold Hariston, also a patron of the coffeehouse then an Air Force Sergeant with the 121st Squadron stationed at McGuire Air Force Base in New Jersey, brought a million dollar suit against Major General Kenneth Collins, individually and as Commanding General of Headquarters, U.S. Army Training, Infantry and Fort Dix, New Jersey; Major Sarah Thompson and "Richard Roe," individually, and in their official capacities, and for all others similarly situated; Paul Schminke, J. Sansone, "John" Parisi, "James" Neil, New Jersey State Trooper Shield Number 2307, individually and in their official capacities as Troopers in the New Jersey State Police and for all others similarly situated; Gerhard P. Dehaas, individually and in his official capacity as a New Jersey State Police Cadet; Colonel David B. Kelley in his capacity as Superintendent of the New Jersey State Police; Nicholas Ferrelli, individually and in his capacity as Chief of Police of Wrightstown; Arthur J. Sills in his capacity as Attorney General of the State of New Jersey.

The plaintiffs brought this suit: "on their own behalf and on behalf of all others similarly situated, namely: (a) those civilians and soldiers in the Fort Dix-Wrightstown, New Jersey area who are involved in political activity opposed to the imperialist policies of the Government, including the war in Vietnam; and (b) those soldiers who have filed or may in the future file application for Conscientious Objector status while in the service; and (c) members of organizations called "dissident" by officials of the United States Army; and (d) all persons frequenting the Fort Dix Coffeehouse; and (e) all persons involved in the writing, publication and distribution of a newspaper called *Shakedown*."

At the suggestion of the Court and with the agreement of the plaintiffs, the action was severed and the claim that the statutes under which they had been jailed were unconstitutional was decided by a three-judge court, while the claims for injunction and damages based on alleged harassment by the defendants would be heard by the judge to whom the case was first presented. The coffeehouse workers won their case on the first part and as of this writing the second part has not been tried.

However, the State Police never gave up trying to close down The Coffeehouse. At one point during the summer of 1969, Beth, Bob, Sam and other workers found out that the Police were going to bust The Coffeehouse by claiming that it was the heroin center of Burlington County. GIs caught on drug charges were being persuaded to sign affidavits stating that they procured their drugs from The Coffeehouse. Many GIs refused and told The Coffeehouse people what was up. The Coffeehouse frowned on drugs. They had enough trouble on their hands without trying anything that risky, aside from the fact that they were against the use of hard drugs. Nevertheless, the State Police bragged that they had twelve signed affidavits and that when they got fifteen they were going to close The Coffeehouse up for good. The Coffeehouse workers countered by inviting townspeople from nearby New Brunswick and Willingborough, and Richard Kilmer from Clergy and Laymen Concerned About Vietnam, to visit The Coffeehouse any time unannounced. People started sending telegrams to the Attorney General of New Jersey and Richard Kilmer held a press conference on the trumped-up charges. In the end, the dope charge never materialized.

On Valentine's Day, February 14, 1970, The Coffeehouse was in full swing. Scores of civilians and soldiers were sitting around the many little tables, talking animatedly, sipping coffee, when the front door opened and a bottle-like object rolled in. Several soldiers recognized the familiar plastic grenade used for training troops at Fort Dix. They ran to throw it out, but the bomb rolled under a coffee machine and exploded before they could get to it. Three soldiers were injured. People ran outside to try and identify the bomb throwers and were shot at by two fleeing men whom they could not identify as they fell to the ground avoiding the bullets. The bomb blew out plywood panels which had recently been nailed down to replace windowpanes smashed in an earlier rock-throwing attack on The Coffeehouse. It took the State Police twenty minutes to arrive on the scene, though they were stationed directly across the street.

The landlord, Michael Schen, who had been patient under pressure, felt he could no longer withstand this kind of violence and The Coffeehouse closed down.

3.

THE DEMONSTRATION

Following the June 5, 1969 stockade riot, The Coffeehouse, the American Servicemen's Union and the Workers Defense League reacted immediately. *Shakedown* featured front-page stories on the riot and the stockade conditions, as did the ASU's newspaper, the *Bond.* The WDL sent out letters to Congressmen and Senators and press releases to the *New York Times, New York Post,* the *Village Voice* and the *Daily News.* A campaign was mounted of "Support Our Brothers in the Pound" but the public at large took little notice.

The Coffeehouse workers came up with the idea of a civilian demonstration on the Fort Dix base.

They invited every peace group and every political group which might conceivably be sympathetic to the cause to join in the planning for the big demonstration. What developed was probably the broadest coalition since the days of the antiwar movement. Everyone joined from the Quakers to the Students for a Democratic Society: the American Servicemen's Union, the Black Panther Party, the Catholic Peace Fellowship, Clergy and Laymen Concerned About Vietnam, the Episcopal Peace Fellowship, Fifth Avenue Peace Parade Committee, Greenwich Village Peace Center, the Law Commune, the Liberation News Service, Lower East Side Mobilization for Peace Action, Movement for a Democratic Society, Newsreel, the Student Mobilization, the United Front Against Fascism, Veterans and Reservists Against the War, Veterans for Peace, Women's Strike for Peace, Young Lords, the Young Patriots (a Chicago-based group of Southern Appalachian white people), and the Young Socialists.

The GIs from The Coffeehouse did most of the footwork. They went out almost every night and spoke on different campuses and addressed various group meetings. Two GIs were able to get passes at this time and they made speaking engagements night and day in Philadelphia and New York and New Jersey. They were eminently successful. In Beth Reisen's words, "We woke up that morning and there were all those people!"

It is interesting to realize that the soldiers and civilians who worked so hard to build the demonstration were surprised

37

by the thousands of civilians who joined them in storming the Army base and that at about the same time the Weathermen who were working toward a huge demonstration to take place in Chicago, in answer to police brutalities at the 1968 Democratic Convention, had no idea of how few people would materialize. They were expecting thousands. It was in planning the demonstration that The Coffeehouse people had their final break with the Weathermen.

Beth detailed the ins and outs of those highly charged meetings:

"Originally the demonstration was scheduled for September 28th. We called a marshal's meeting before the demonstration and people came from all over. The Weathermen sent down their whole New York collective, about forty people. They made up about one-third of the entire meeting. Most groups just sent representatives. At this meeting we were going to discuss what we thought would be the best way to run this demonstration. These representatives would be marshals, would know what our plan was and would so direct the people. We decided that the march would start at Wrightstown with the older people who were not into militant action at the front of the line, and head straight for the gates of Fort Dix. The other people would divide into two groups and veer off along the railroad tracks and go in across the field, which in fact is where we did go in the end.

"The Weathermen had fits. They wanted the most militant people up in front. They insisted that that was the only way you can achieve anything and that, 'You don't tell people what they're getting into. We'll just lead them in. We'll break through the MP lines. We'll get into the stockade. We'll do this, we'll do that and any GI that tries to stop us is a PIG.' Their whole thing was calling the GIs pigs, fighting the GIs. We said that can't be, that would destroy everything we've worked for. It would be totally counterproductive to any organizing we could do at Dix. This is to be a demonstration to support GIs, to encourage organizing on base, to build support for the Fort Dix Thirty-Eight. What you people are saying doesn't make any sense. They insisted they were coming anyway and they were going to do it their way. The other bone of contention was that they wanted NLF flags at the front of the line and we said that a lot of guys who had fought in Nam have a sensitive reaction to NLF flags. [The Philadelphia group actually threatened to withdraw at this point when the Weathermen insisted on carrying the flags.] So we said nope, no carrying flags, no fighting the GIs. They said, 'We're going to come anyhow and we're going to bring the flags.' We said, 'Okay, no demonstration.' That was a real horror show. Everyone was very upset. All the other groups supported us but didn't want to hear us say, 'No demonstration.'

"The Weathermen called up the next day and said they'd leave their NLF flags at home. We said that wasn't really the heart of the issue. We postponed the demonstration for two weeks when the Weathermen would be in Chicago. It worked out beautifully. As October 12th approached, our organizing became regional. We had representatives from New York, Philadelphia, New Jersey, New Haven, and Boston, and a few representatives at large. We had them elect a tactical leadership who then worked out the final plans.

"Two days before the demonstration we had a meeting with the tactical leadership, about ten people, and the most trusted of our GIs and the most trusted of our civilian Coffeehouse workers. Oddly enough we later found out that MPs who were brought from Fort Meade to help control the demonstrators for the Army were briefed on details. They told us they had been informed by the Army that our demonstration was going to be led by women, that many of them might be wearing helmets (which we had talked about), that the women at the very front might carry poles to hold the front line together [the poles were used]. They just knew everything we had talked about, so that either we had an informer in our meeting of very select tactical advisors, or we were bugged, which is what I suspect.

"It was interesting that we decided to have women lead the demonstration, because one of the hardest things to talk about to GIs, we found out, was women's liberation, more so than racism or communism, the white soldiers' two fears. So many guys would say initially, 'We're in Vietnam to stop communism.' *What's Communism?* 'Communism is when the government makes you do what you don't want to.' *Are you in the Army?* 'Yeah.' *Do you want to be in the Army?* 'No.' *Well then?* Or, *What's Communism?* 'Communism is where everyone has to dress alike, eat alike and do what the government tells them to do.' *The Army?* 'Yeah, the Army's Communist.' So many times . . . But women's liberation is particularly hard for them to accept because it's the one area where most of these guys feel any power at all."

Where the GIs overcame their distrusts and agreed to women leading the demonstration on the other side of the military fence, it turned out that the Fort Dix officers had their distrusts. Unlike the GIs they didn't overcome them. They distrusted their own Military Police.

In Beth's words: "They couldn't trust their own MPs at Fort Dix. They didn't call out any of the 759th Military Police battalion until the very end of the demonstration. They kept them restricted in the barracks. They brought special riot troops all the way from Fort Meade, Maryland and Fort Bragg, North Carolina. The Dix guards were too sympathetic. Many of them had been reading *Shakedown*. Many of the 759th battalion were not MPs by choice. They had spent their year in Vietnam and were assigned MP duty for six months or a year until they got out. Some of the best people that we had come in contact with have been from the 759th Military Police battalion. This was one reason why we said you just can't call MPs pigs. It's just not true. Some of them used to do very fine things in the stockade. They don't have the 759th in the stockade anymore."

Herbert Dreyer, who had helped found The Coffeehouse is a short, thoughtful student with deep brown eyes and electric Einsteinian hair. He was the co-chairman of the demonstration meeting and one of the chief speakers at the demonstration. He recalled the initial coalition meeting for the demonstration in even more detail than Beth:

"Everything bad about the Movement came out in that meeting. Nobody talked to each other as human beings. Nobody saw the situation realistically which was that whenever the Army wanted to stop us, they could stop us. There was no question that we could ever get to the stockade. That was a projected goal, but to assume that was to assume that the base would just melt away. We explained this reality to the Weathermen and other militants. They refused to believe it. They said, 'We'll fight it through.' We suggested that the march split up in three ways, which also turned out to be unrealistic, but that was like a tentative thing, so that each group would be able to function in their own way and not be interfered with by another group whom normally they would hate. The pacifists would do a vigil at one end; the theatre people would talk or do plays and also this would spread out the march so that they literally would have to surround the base with troops and make them use as many troops as they had to maximize our contact with them. But they didn't see that at all. There was one guy named Ron Carver who was chairing the meeting with me. He had been in the Movement probably longer than anyone at that meeting. He had faced Ku Klux Klansmen with shotguns in the South, in Mississippi, for a year when some of these Weathermen were in junior high school. Ron said: 'Look, I've done other things. Why don't you at least listen to what I say on the basis of my record. Just listen.' They said: 'Then you were right on and now you're right off.' They had their line. In the meeting, Philly Resistance and other groups in Philadelphia said that if it was going to be a violent demonstration they would withdraw.

"We said to the Weathermen: 'Look, you're really causing a lot of damage here.' And they said: 'It's immaterial whether an 80-year-old Quaker woman gets killed or a massacre occurs if the point of the demonstration is made,' something like that. They were totally heartless. They announced that the GIs had nothing to do with the demonstration anymore, The Coffeehouse had nothing to do with it. The Weathermen were having the demonstration and to follow their lead because they were the vanguard. So we called off the demonstration which shocked people in our own group. We made the decision on the spot and there were lots of disagreements because we were trying to defend the men in the stockade and people thought any demonstration would be better than none. This would look like a mess and it would hurt the feelings of the men in the stockade. So we called it for a time when the Weathermen would be in Chicago. Everyone would have a choice as to what part of the movement they wanted to relate to. This sort of dispute continued all the way through the demonstration up until the last. The night before the Dix demonstration, at 4:00 A.M., when there was a split in the Weathermen and the people who left the Weathermen became the Mad Dogs, the Weathermen still wanted to have the militant demonstration—even after it was announced that it was going to be peaceful. Finally we just asserted control. We said: 'Forget it,' and wouldn't let them have anything to do with the demonstration and they relented."

Herb also recalled that there was one group in the coalition that people tend to forget: "There was a group of bikers from surrounding areas [of Fort Dix], like Browns Mills which is a little town on the other side of the base from Wrightstown, a very quiet residential place, and from Mt. Holly, who joined in. There are a lot of bikers in and around Wrightstown. They're greasers, with long hair, Hell's Angels types, with leather jackets and all the accouterments. Maybe twenty or thirty. We really don't know. They came to Beth before the demonstration; they heard there was going to be a demo and they said

41

that they didn't like the Army. So they got a map of the back of Fort Dix and at the time of the demonstration they tried to ride their bikes through the woods and barnstorm the base. They were going to charge through the stockade on their bikes. But they got hung up in some trees and barbed wire. Apparently the Army really put up barbed wire all around the base and woods. But they tried to do it and it was interesting because at that time the Weathermen's thing was to try and build up a coalition with greasers, disenfranchised street people so to speak, with which they had no success. Ours was the first project where these people just came on their own. It was organic. It reinforced our belief that you really don't organize people; you say something and if it appeals to people they join in."

First, on October 8th, there was a small demonstration in New York City to build support for the larger one. Several hundred people gathered at Penn Station for a rally, then marched down Eighth Avenue to Twenty-Fourth Street and regrouped in front of a government building which housed recruiting stations for all the military services. GIs from The Coffeehouse who knew the stockade conditions firsthand addressed the demonstrators both at Penn Station and in front of the government building. They presented the four demands which had become the rallying cry for the Fort Dix demonstration: FREE THE FORT DIX THIRTY-EIGHT! ABOLISH THE STOCKADE SYSTEM! FREE ALL POLITICAL PRISONERS, HUEY NEWTON, BOBBY SEALE, THE PANTHER TWENTY-ONE! IMMEDIATE WITHDRAWAL OF UNITED STATES OCCUPATION FORCES FROM VIETNAM!

When the long-awaited October 12th finally dawned, it was a perfect Indian summer Sunday. Hundreds of buses and cars started arriving at The Coffeehouse. A gray haze lay over Wrightstown and just as the sun made its welcome appearance so did a rock band of musicians from Fort Dix and nearby McGuire Air Force Base. The band played with great gusto as people kept arriving from states as disparate as South Carolina and New Hampshire and from a host of universities—from Princeton, Drew, Rutgers, Wesleyan, Columbia and NYU. The turnout was staggering.

Around noon Herb Dreyer read the "Support Our GIs" statement and discussed the four demands in detail. A member of the Quaker Action group told of the enthusiastic reception they had received on their long walk from Philadelphia to

Maryland and an airborne division from Fort Bragg, North Carolina—this last division they hid overnight in the woods."

In their mysterious way the military officers seem to have been moved by the demonstrators. Lieutenant Colonel P. J. Neelon was quoted by several newspapers as having said: "To my knowledge this is the first time in the history of America that civilians have forced their way onto a military base for the purpose of a demonstration." Of the demonstrators he said: "They sure organized a hell of a fine march."

In retrospect, the stockade conditions at Fort Dix gained public notice not because of the torturing of prisoners, nor the inhumane overcrowded conditions in the stockade, not because two hundred and fifty men rioted in the stockade—since this desperate uprising barely grazed the public's attention—nor because thirty-eight of these home-based soldiers were threatened with courts-martial. In the end Fort Dix became famous in 1969 because thousands of civilians demonstrated on an Army base.

That one October afternoon's demonstration penetrated the thicket of silence that was rapidly engulfing the riot and the base. The confrontation between thousands of unarmed civilians and one thousand gas-masked, bayonet-pushing militia fixed Fort Dix in the public's mind and imagination.

Wrightstown. Kathy Russell, Jeff Russell's wife, who had a sign taped to her back "Free My Husband!" spoke of the importance of the demonstration to the men in the stockade. She said that when she last saw Jeff, he didn't have to tell her anything about the way they were treating him. He had lost sixty pounds. Other people spoke, Young Lords, Young Patriots and Black Panthers. Barbara Dane sang resistance ballads and dedicated one song to the helicopter planes that were circling overhead.

Finally the demonstration got moving, marching eight abreast through the main streets of Wrightstown, stretching further than the eye could see, chanting "Free the Fort Dix Thirty-Eight!" "The brass lives high while GIs die!" "Power to the People!" Army helicopters lowered over the marchers as they turned up Fort Dix Street, then right on Main Street. All the honky-tonk Army pawn stores were boarded up. Onlooking townies gawked at the spectacle of their streets choked with singing, chanting marchers. The marchers called out, "Join us!" An occasional bystander did join. A few window watchers gave V signs from their windows. All the formal entrances to the base were fenced off with barbed wire and a freshly painted sign faced the demonstrators as they approached the base: WARNING! UNAUTHORIZED DEMONSTRATIONS PROHIBITED. Ignoring this sign and finding an open space, the helmeted women's brigade veered across a grassy field and headed for the stockade. They carried rolled-up rugs to throw over the barbed wire barricade surrounding the detention area. Soon thousands of civilians surged onto the base backing up the women's brigade.

Colonel Herman Carr, the Provost Marshal in charge of the military police, boomed a warning through his bull horn: "This is to advise you that you are in violation of Federal law and if you persist you will be arrested." The demonstrators drowned him out with their chanted demands. Seconds later hundreds of gas-masked soldiers came running toward the demonstrators, pushing bayonet-tipped rifles in front of them. They faced the front line of women. There were some skirmishes as the demonstrators tried to outflank the line of soldiers. More soldiers arrived. The chanting grew louder. By 3:00 there were one thousand armed soldiers confronting the demonstrators. Some of the women spoke to soldiers telling them that they were on their side, explaining their mission, asking the gas-masked creatures to drop their guns and masks. Colonel Carr reappeared and boomed: "You are in violation of Federal law. If you do not disperse, we will have to use tear gas. Go back to the road. We will have to use chemical agents."

Andrew Stapp, founder and chairman of the American Servicemen's Union, shouted a message through his bull horn back to the MPs: "You're just being used against your brothers in the pound. Do you want to be sent to Vietnam? Have any of you guys been court-martialed? You know what the fucking court-martial system is like." Colonel Carr gave the order to fire and the gas-masked soldiers hurled tear bombs into the middle of the civilian group. At first the wind blew the stinging choking gas back towards the guards, but more bombs were hurled by the advancing soldiers and the civilians beat a hasty retreat. About forty people were treated by the demonstrators' medical team, but there were no serious injuries and no arrests.

Margaret Meister, a young pacifist who had worked with A. S. Neill at Summerhill and had participated in a nonviolent workshop in Philadelphia, and who with Herb, Beth, Sam, and others helped create The Coffeehouse and the demonstration, checked up on the tear gas as several people were having bad lingering aftereffects four days after the demonstration: "I called up the Army Information. They said that it was CS gas. We had also gotten information from Dr. Richard Kunnes. He's a psychiatrist and he works with Health-Pac and the Medical Commission on Human Rights and he had sent us information about the different gases. Some of it was pretty gory. CN gas is enough to dispel any group of people. That's what we usually call tear gas; it stings, it makes your eyes tear and it makes you cough and cry and you can't breathe properly. But CS gas has burning elements which make your skin very hot and it's like an intense burning sensation, especially on your face. It has nausea elements too which can cause severe vomiting."

Both Herbert Dreyer and Margaret Meister felt that the use of gas and the restricting of men on base was counterproductive for the Army. As Herbert put it: "There was a possibility that the restriction of the men on base would make them, the GIs, angry at the demonstrators because they had to stay on the base, but it worked the opposite way. They were just angry at the brass. Many GIs who were at the demonstration itself were very impressed and came up to The Coffeehouse afterwards and told us that they agreed with us and they were against the war too. The men who did the tear gassing itself, they said they were from Fort Bragg, and that the next time they would gas the sergeants. They were actually gassed themselves because the masks didn't shield them, so it went right back in their faces and they were angry at the use of this gas.

"The tear gassing outraged the townspeople. Word appar-

ently went back to town and they brought buckets of [w...] to help take off the gas. This was while we were st[...] the field. That was an extraordinary gesture. Even the [...] worked in the MacDonald's hamburger stand, who wou[...] even speak to us before, said that everyone was i[...] that the demonstration was so peaceful and friendly."

Leroi Conley, a self-assured black soldier, remem[...] day of the demonstration from a deeper vantage poin[...] Leroi's Army duty had taken him from the occupat[...] in Germany to the Special Detachment Forces at Fort [...] he was trying to get a release as a hardship case. [...] had suffered an injury on her job, had become para[...] could no longer support her three children.

He told about that October 12th with great emot[...] the demonstration came, the October 12th demonstra[...] of us could participate in it, but the support behind [...] was just incredible, especially my particular uni[...] Special Troops. It was a replacement company, [...] returning from Vietnam who still had some duty to d[...] waiting to be transferred to another unit; or guys li[...] hardship cases waiting to get mustered out or waiti[...] passionate reassignments. Everybody else's unit [...] what restricted to the base. Our unit was restrict[...] to the base but to the barracks and not only to the [...] some of us were restricted to our rooms. We coul[...] So we stuck out the windows and gave fists an[...] The only thing that I regret was that nobody else c[...] support. There were a lot of civilians out there r[...] into it, but they just couldn't see the support that w[...] further in the base. Throughout the whole base[...] nothing but 'Right on!' and cheers and there were [...] waving."

At the end of the day the demonstrators were [...] choking, and sneezing. They regrouped one last [...] way 68 to hear Herbert Dreyer sum up the dem[...] pronounced through his bull horn: "We have m[...] We have scored victories! Three hundred and si[...] ers have been released from the stockade today [...] civilian demonstration. A detachment of Absent [...] prisoners have been given passes for the day, w[...] happened before at Dix. The 'brass' has impris[...] base, restricting the GIs so they could not join u[...] stration. They even restricted the 759th MP b[...] place they flew in riot-trained military police fr[...]

44

45

4.
THE TRIALS AND THE FIVE YOUNG MEN

After the riot, when thirty-eight young men chosen by the CID from hundreds of rioters were being caged, starved and chained, a planeload of USA representatives flew halfway round the world to report on tiger cages in Vietnam. Had they visited the Fort Dix stockade these government officials might have been startled to see Bill Brakefield, Tom Catlow, Terry Klug, Jeff Russell and Carlos Rodriguez Torres chained to chairs, to hear first-hand reports of the starvings, beatings and of the leather straps used on young Americans not yet proved innocent or guilty.

The five young men chosen to suffer the same bitter fate, awaiting courts-martial in Disciplinary Seg, came from utterly disparate backgrounds. By the time of the riot they were all dead set against the war in Vietnam. Yet each young man had originally enlisted in the Army at a very young age with very different hopes and feelings. Their stories and their trials are as singular as the men themselves.

JEFFREY RUSSELL

The conviction of Jeffrey Russell is a shocking example of the flaws in our system of military justice. Although there is no credible evidence that Private Russell had committed any crime, he was convicted and sentenced to three years at hard labor.

It is evident to me that his conviction was based on the Army's effort to protect its own image, and to maintain discipline, regardless of the means it has to employ. I have never seen anything like it in my twenty years of law practice.

The continued disregard by the Army of the most rudimentary standards of due process can only encourage the young people of this country to have contempt for an institution which, in order to suppress any criticism or dissent, will select and mistreat scapegoats.

—Judith Vladeck, co-counsel
for Jeffrey Russell

The first to be tried was Jeffrey Russell. Jeffrey's trial for alleged participation in the stockade riot of June 5, 1969 finally got started on November 9, 1969. That first day of that first Fort Dix riot trial had an air of suspense about it hard to recapture. The civilian sympathizers, the silent protesters, the milling media didn't know what to expect.

This court-martial and those to follow were held in a small, low, one-room, yellow brick building with a very limited seating capacity. The squat building had no air of high drama. It was hard to believe, at first, that a young man was being tried for a possible sentence of fifty years in so casual a place. Inside, MPs with helmets and guns leaned at ease against a wall. Relaxed soldiers in different uniforms moved about, chatting with lawyers and assorted civilians. The low-ceilinged room had the comic air of a Woody Allen "banana republic" until the entry of the "Court" (jury in civilian terms). These military officers with their singularly unsmiling faces, stiff bearing and rigid limbs changed the tenor of the place. It was then the audience sensed that the twenty-year-old Private, Jeffrey Russell, was going to have no easy time of it.

Jeffrey, of medium height and on the slight side, has a quick mind and an engaging way about him; bright brown eyes,

48

a small straight nose, clear skin, always neat in appearance. Jeffrey, an omnivorous reader, loves conversation and has a vivid imagination.

Jeffrey was born in New Burn, North Carolina, September 20, 1949. His father is a retired Lieutenant Commander in the Navy. Jeff has a brother two years and three months older and a sister who was born on his eighth birthday. The Russells would move every year or two. Jeff was educated in private schools in North Carolina, New Jersey, Florida and Virginia. He was a good student but a restive human being. His father's authoritarian attitude rankled Jeff: "My father would give us the 'white glove' inspection in the morning, bells ringing, the whole business. I reacted strongly with the feeling that I wanted to get away." At seventeen Jeffrey applied to William and Mary College but because of his strong desire to get away: "I joined the Army, of all ridiculous things. I was only seventeen. I wasn't thinking politically yet, or of pacifism. I had read a lot of philosophy but it had never occurred to me to apply these readings to my own behavior. When I joined the Army they offered me Army Security Agency, top secret security clearance, and that was glamorous to me then. To get into ASA you had to be a high school graduate and you had to pass a battery of tests with high scores; as a result most of the men were college students who hadn't finished college and decided that the Army would pay the rest of the way. The ASA was the intelligence elite of the Army. I enlisted in Richmond, Virginia, took Basic at Fort Jackson, South Carolina and then went to Fort Devens, Massachusetts for my training."

They were going to train Jeffrey first as a traffic analyst and then as a crypt analyst. The former receives codes and breaks them with the help of a code book; the latter breaks codes for which there are no known keys. It was at Fort Devens that Jeffrey says, "I first began to think for myself. I was trying to get away from parental authority and here I was in the middle of military authority which was much worse; but I had joined of my own free will and from my point of view then I was obligated to stick out my time in the Army. I had signed up for four years.

"There were liberals, radicals and pacifists in the ASA and I had friends in the resistance movement in Boston. I was beginning to question the war in Vietnam myself and all the military premises I had taken over from my parents. And then one day I realized that I couldn't go to Vietnam. At that time

I was still naive enough to think that they were going to allow me some free choice in this matter.

"I went to the Captain, my company commander and told him how I felt. He said, 'You know what you'll do. You'll go where we send you.' I decided to go AWOL that weekend just for the weekend and ended up staying a week."

Jeff was eighteen when he went AWOL for the first time. He traveled around Boston to Harvard and MIT investigating for himself what the dissent to the war in Vietnam was all about. When he returned to Fort Devons he was court-martialed and put in the stockade for three months. He was then dismissed from the ASA school and sent to Fort Dix. At Fort Dix he was to be trained as a light weapons infantry man. Jeff explained to his CO that he had become a pacifist and could not fight in any war.

"This CO was just back from Vietnam. He had risen through the ranks. He was a sergeant, field promotion and, oh God, did he ever jump on me. He told me they were going to court-martial me and throw me in the stockade. After my three months in the Fort Devons stockade I certainly didn't want to go back in, so I went AWOL again, this time to New York.

"I worked for NBC and Countrywide and did some free-lance writing. I went to seminars at the New School and at NYU. I was trying to work as a writer and an actor. I met some people who had been to Philip Kaplow's Rochester Meditation Center and I knew a Buddhist Master, Shaky Ghitan. I started to meditate and became a Buddhist."

That spring while studying to be an actor Jeff met a young actress, Kathy Cormack. They fell in love and got married on September 20, 1968. Jeff had been doing some draft counseling and had talked before casual groups. Though he wasn't officially connected with any peace group he had friends in many of them and he was asked by his friends to address the big peace rally at Sheeps Meadow in Central Park during the summer of 1968. He spoke about his pacifist convictions and told the young people what it was like to be in the Army. Jeff thinks that the FBI or CIA or CID traced him from the Sheeps Meadow rally.

The following January (1969) Jeff worked with a group that was trying to get jobs for Czechoslovakian refugees. He became the manager of a restaurant on the east side which hired Czechs as busboys, dishwashers, cooks and waitresses. A waitress told the owner that Jeff was letting his friends smoke dope late at night in the restaurant. The owner phoned the police and as Jeff remembered it: "They were sitting waiting when this friend of mine came in. He had nothing on him. I don't know whether it was because of this, or because the Army was tracking me down but early the next morning while Kathy and I were still asleep two narcotics agents came by my place."

According to Jeff one agent placed some marijuana with hashish in it while the other agent held a gun to Kathy and himself. He and Kathy were taken down to the Tombs, were fingerprinted and then released on their own recognizance. The young Russells were sure that the FBI would be at Jeff's door to arrest him for desertion within the next few days and the question was whether to go to Canada or stay. "We decided we would stay and get it over with because we thought that at most I'd serve six months in the stockade, then I'd get a discharge and that would be the end of it." Kathy was three months pregnant.

The FBI came by two days later. They took Jeff straight to the stockade at Dix. At first they had his records confused with someone else's. They thought he was a blonde, blue-eyed Sergeant who had just come from a hospital and was mentally unstable. The only things they had right were his fingerprints and his name. His records had gone to Indianapolis. When they got it straightened out, according to Jeffrey, they labeled him a communist.

Jeffrey made three strong statements while in the Dix stockade. Explaining his second AWOL which landed him in Dix, Jeff said: "I left because I could not support the war, violence or the atrocities committed in the name of freedom and Christ." On July 24, 1968, after his conviction and sentencing to two years for AWOL, he wrote: "I am a political prisoner here at Fort Dix. If I may quote Henry David Thoreau, 'The only obligation which I have a right to assume is to do at any time what I think is right.' By acting thus I support my country as well as humanity. To quote Thoreau again, I could not stay in the Army because I could not, 'lend myself to the evil which I condemn,' so for exercising my 'freedom of thought and action' I got two years." The last statement came in answer to questions about his Buddhist faith: "I think all religions are universal. They all believe in peace and I still have faith in nonviolence. If it's antisocial to kill one man, what could be more antisocial than a war? If I sat down to rap with General Westmoreland he wouldn't pick up a gun and shoot me if he disagreed with what I was saying. But that's just what war is."

51

When the riot took place on June 5th, 1969, Jeffrey was awaiting a Post decision on his two-year sentence from his court-martial for AWOL. While in the stockade Jeffrey had joined the American Servicemen's Union. Russell was a particular butt of the stockade guards. They had heard of his father, the Lieutenant Commander in the Navy, and they despised Jeffrey's Buddhism and pacifism. The day he was put in segregation they confiscated a tiny ivory Buddha that held a double significance for Jeffrey. He used it for meditation and it had been given to him by Kathy. They never returned the Buddha. Jeffrey was badly beaten by the guards six times while in confinement. Besides being the special target of the guards, Jeffrey was the man singled out by the CID. They chose to bring extra pressure on him to testify against his fellow prisoners on a variety of charges. Like a modern Job, Jeff bore the added burden of parents-in-law who refused to help support their daughter and tried to get custody of their grandchild. Then to top it off his own mother wrote him excoriating letters denouncing his behavior. The day he was placed in Segregation for alleged participation in the riot, Kathy gave birth to their son, Jeffrey Jr. The Army refused to recognize the reality of a Buddhist marriage so Kathy never received any payments for medical expenses.

Toward the end of her pregnancy Kathy was penniless. Jeffrey, along with all other stockade prisoners, received no pay. Kathy had to quit her job. Her last resort was to go home to her parents in Raleigh, North Carolina and have her baby there. She knew her parents disapproved of her marriage. Her father, W. J. Cormack, was the engineer manager of Zenith and very pro-war at the time. After Kathy gave birth to Jeff Jr., Mr. Cormack received a letter from Lieutenant Commander Russell informing him that Jeffrey was accused of arson, conspiracy to riot, riot, and destruction of government property and that— equally shameful—he was being defended by Rowland Watts whom the Lieutenant Commander understood to be a "Communist lawyer." Kathy remembers those days as among the worst she suffered: "I had no money. I was worried about Jeff and had no news. My parents took the baby away from me as soon as I came home from the hospital." But Kathy is a resourceful young woman and she fought back: "I went to the Senator from North Carolina, Senator Everett B. Jordan. He and his secretary were just wonderful to me. They gave me money and helped me to get the baby back which finally ended in a lawsuit in my favor. I don't know how many times

52

they called Fort Dix for me, but they arranged to have the Chaplain there marry Jeff and me in a ceremony that the Army would recognize so that the baby and I could receive our benefits. They gave me additional funds to go to Dix with the baby."

When Kathy arrived at Fort Dix, Chaplain Mallow, who had agreed over the phone to Senator Jordan to marry the Russells, refused. Kathy turned to Rowland Watts of the Workers Defense League, who at that time was the civilian attorney for all the alleged conspirators. Kathy says that the only person who helped her in those early days at Dix was Rowland and that he went all over the place trying to find a chaplain to marry the Russells. It seems that Army chaplains don't consider that Buddhists can be married under the eyes of "Their Lord." Just when Rowland Watts was beginning to despair of the whole project he was put in touch with a highly unorthodox man of the cloth who had the necessary credentials. So on July 20, 1969, Jeffrey and Kathy Russell were remarried in the Fort Dix stockade chapel by Sam, the Priest.

Kathy and the baby had been staying at the enlisted men's guest house and one evening when she came back to her room she found her clothes strewn all over the room and liquor spilled on her bed. She went running to Rowland who took her over to The Coffeehouse and introduced her to the young people there. Kathy says that she was still naive politically and had heard that they were Communists, and Communists to her were terrifying people. But as soon as she met Saul Shapiro and Beth Reisen she realized they were young friendly people like herself. And from then on she says, "They took care of me and the baby. My family wouldn't give me any support whatsoever."

Before the court-martial, at the 39A hearing (the equivalent of a civilian pre-trial hearing) on October 13, 1969, defense attorney Rowland Watts of the Workers Defense League, his co-counsel Judith Vladeck and Curtis McClane submitted seven motions to dismiss Jeffrey Russell's charges.

The first motion was an effort to disqualify the trial counsel, Captain Ross Anzaldi, because of his previous confidential relationship with Jeffrey. Captain Anzaldi, a tall, dark aspiring Army lawyer, who was to serve as Jeff's prosecutor, had figured prominently as Terry Klug's defense counsel on April 18, 1969, in his court-martial on charges of desertion. Captain Anzaldi was then a Lieutenant. Both Terry Klug and Jeffrey Russell claimed they had talked to Captain Anzaldi confidentially about the riot, not dreaming he was going to figure as prosecutor in any of the riot trials. Terry Klug claimed that he had specifically discussed the CID (Criminal Investigation Division) attempts to bribe witnesses with Captain Anzaldi and that: "Captain Anzaldi called Jeff in and asked him how things were going. Jeff told him that he was on rather dangerous charges and would like to know if Captain Anzaldi would consider taking his case. The Captain said he would consider it and asked Jeff to fill him in on a few details. After Captain Anzaldi assured Jeff that he would not be acting as trial counsel on this case or on any of the riot cases, Jeff agreed to tell the Captain what he knew. A few months later we were informed that this same Captain Anzaldi had been assigned to prosecute three of the five cases in General Court."

Specialist 4 Robert W. Alstrom 532nd Military Police Battalion, the guard who had escorted Jeffrey to the JAG (Judge Advocate General) office in June after the riot, remembered Jeffrey discussing the stockade conditions with Captain Anzaldi. He recalled Jeff complained of being in Segregation, complained that the CID was bribing witnesses to testify against him, that he had been put on DS chow . . . and he remembered Jeff declaring that he asked Captain Anzaldi if he would be his defense counsel and Captain Anzaldi said he didn't know if he could or not. Specialist Alstrom also testified that the conversation lasted about fifteen minutes.

The motion to disqualify Captain Ross Anzaldi as trial counsel was denied. A motion was also denied to dismiss the proceedings because of special interest on the part of the investigating officer in the 32 hearing. An Army 32 hearing is equivalent to a Grand Jury prima facie hearing in civilian courts. Captain Robert W. Worthing by his own testimony had been assigned to keep records of the thirty-eight men accused of participating in the riot and he had been instrumental in deciding which of these men would be let off and which of them would go to trial. Then in Jeffrey Russell's case he became the presiding officer to review the case and decide whether Jeffrey should be given a court-martial, a Gilbert and Sullivan redundancy of functions on the part of Captain Worthing. He had been asked by Attorney Watts to disqualify himself from the 32 proceedings, but had refused.

But of all the motions to be brought up in the 39A hearing the most salient to Jeffrey's immediate experience, the most revelatory of the stockade conditions, was motion number six. This motion was an effort to bar the trial on grounds of prior punishment. A proffer of proof was made to show that Russell was subjected to both harassment and solicitation to commit perjury by CID agents on June 6th; that from June 7th to June 9th he was held in Disciplinary Segregation, deprived of all rights, held incommunicado without any legal charges, held strictly because of his reputation; that from June 9th up until and including the day that these motions were being put forth (October 13), he was being held in Disciplinary Segregation, which meant in fact having his bunk stripped of its mattress and having to sit for sixteen hours a day every day on the steel or wooden bunk; that he was denied the right to attend religious movies, or any other privileges; that he had been attacked twice by guards with the acquiescence of administrative officers; that on one such attack his hands had been shackled behind his back; that his outgoing mail had been read contrary to the Army's own regulations and that some of it had been improperly returned to him; that his incoming mail of a privileged nature, contrary to the Army's own regulations, had been read; that for a period of time he was denied his right to communicate with his attorney—again against the Army's own regulations; that visiting rights of his friend Saul Shapiro were taken away from him; that his wife Kathy had been harassed and humiliated repeatedly on the post and at the stockade and that her visiting rights had been severely curtailed; that Jeffrey had been denied the solace of his religion, in that his little ivory Buddha had been taken away from him and he had been denied consultation with a Buddhist priest or Lama; that his religious rights had been further impinged upon in that he had been denied the right to participate in the only religious services available in the stockade, that of the Protestant or Catholic faiths; that his 5-10 requests had been either improperly processed or totally ignored, again contrary to the Army's own regulations; that he was required to sign for a handbook, to which all prisoners are entitled and which he was never given (the handbook apprised prisoners of their rights and the Army's regulations for prisoners), that with the acquiescence of the stockade authorities he had been continually harassed and taunted including being the butt of abusive language by the prison guards and officers.

The Judge Advocate, Colonel Thomas J. Nichols, denied this motion on the authority of the U.S. vs. Vaughn 11CMR 121, adding the comment that if the Vaughn case was bad law, which he personally doubted, it was up to the Court of Military Appeals to say so.

The seventh motion was made to dismiss all charges on the grounds that the accused had been denied his statutory rights to a speedy trial and that this had not only resulted in the prolonged punishment before the accused had been proven innocent or guilty but had resulted in serious harm to the building of a defense through the disappearance of successive witnesses and the successive replacement of defense counsels. At least eight witnesses had become unavailable, through AWOL or discharge and it was brought to the attention of Judge Nichols that the original counsel for the defense, Captain Vercimak, had been transferred to Vietnam, that Captain Sklar who then took up the defense had become a judge at Courts and Boards and that Captain Scanlon had only been appointed to the case in the latter weeks. This motion was denied. Rowland Watts then moved for immediate trial, stating that the defense was ready. Judge Nichols consulted his diary and suggested the week of November 3rd. Rowland Watts protested the delay.

For many Easterners Russell's trial was their initiation into military justice first hand and for Judith Vladeck, a labor attorney who had no previous experience with the military, it was a revelation: "I don't know to this day whether I regret it [being Jeffrey Russell's co-counsel in his court-martial] or not. It changed my life very substantially. It was one of the most painful experiences I've ever had." Her experience of the trial is important because Judith Vladeck is particularly sensitive to political partisanship in legal practice, as she revealed:
"For many years I had felt that every lawyer has an obligation to give some percentage of time to free work. I had been a member of the Board of Directors of the New York Civil Liberties Union. I had differences with the approach that they took in politicizing their activities. I have the greatest concern about constitutional rights and defending constitutional rights. For instance, I am concerned about free speech. It is as important to me that George Lincoln Rockwell have a right to speak freely as someone whose views I may accept or subscribe to. I found that the Union was getting to a point where it was saying well, the good guys have the right to speak and as for the bad guys there is no due process. I could no longer work with them. There's only one other organization that I know of that does provide legal service to persons who are involved in cases where there is a deprivation of first amendment rights or other constitutionally protected rights, and that

is the WDL. After my work with ACLU had ended I told Rowland Watts of WDL that I was available to assist in any case in which I might be useful. I had not selected military cases at all. As it turned out my offer was timed pretty closely to the Dix cases and he asked me to help with the defense of Jeffrey Russell.

"I have practiced in all kinds of law, primarily labor law, for more than twenty years. The most exciting thing about labor law is that it is varied. With this training behind me I had absolutely no trepidation about appearing in military court. I thought I was prepared by my varied practice, but I was terribly wrong. There is something about a military court for which one is not prepared by any experience in the civilian world. I think the primary difference is the total lack of courtesy to the defense counsel. We have been pariahs before. My husband and I represented an officer of the Communist Party in New York . . . when he had been denied unemployment benefits. We went into courtrooms where people turned their backs, so that I have been accustomed to people identifying us with whatever our clients' interests might be at the moment; but I had never yet encountered a situation in which attorneys were not given the opportunity for conferring privately with their clients, for recesses in order to prepare for the next step in the presentations of their cases, for the total lack of consideration for the rights of counsel which of course have to effect the rights of the accused.

"We were very short of assistance in the Russell case. On the first day I had taken my college-aged son to Fort Dix, partly because the trip was a painfully long one and he could share the driving and partly because this was a case in which he was very interested. On the second day of the trial the court interfered with the rights of spectators by filling every row for spectators in the courtroom with soldiers whom they brought in. They only kept one row free for the public and the press. My son had been taking notes for me as the public relations officer learned on the first day. By the second day and the third day as tempers began to fray, the P.R. officer began to deny my son access to the courtroom because he said there was a shortage of space and he warned him that if he lost his seat and left to get coffee for anyone he would not be permitted to return. The Russell case went on for several days and I came from New York each day. I had not asked for any indulgence because of this, but the opportunity for talking to Jeff and the opportunity for talking to my co-counsel was so limited as to be almost punitive. The request for a few minutes recess was not granted.

"There was one funny episode. It was a miserable weekend, rain and sleet. The roads were frosted. I had a coughing spell in the courtroom. I was coughing as if I would choke. In a normal courtroom the judge would ask if you want a moment's recess and the other counsel would be courteous enough to offer a glass of water. In this military courtroom they all looked away as if I were creating an unpleasant disturbance which they had to put up with but they certainly weren't going to do anything about it. I have never seen anything like that anywhere in the world. I am told that this is standard procedure in a military court in America.

"I was not prepared for the attitude of the military judge. For pure sadism, I don't think I have ever seen anything to equal his interruption of the trial on the Friday afternoon in which the testimony had been completed and the arguments in litigation had been completed. I had been informed that the normal procedure was that as soon as that stage had been reached the jury would be excused and the jury would come back with its verdict. Abruptly at 4:00 P.M., it may have been a little earlier than 4:00, Colonel Nichols stood up and said: 'The court is in recess until 9:00 o'clock Monday morning,' which meant that this poor youngster Jeff and his wife had a whole weekend in which to sweat out the verdict. I asked without recalling that I was in a military court: 'Is that necessary? Isn't it possible for them to retire now?' And the judge said: 'No, we've had too long a day.' There was no excuse, unless the jury was to get instructions from some other source which is too paranoid a thought. That was just a needless bit of cruelty. Jeff and Kathy had gone through an emotional storm. Kathy is a seriously disturbed girl, as you know; for that child to have had the forty-eight or fifty hours of strain was totally unnecessary. I came away feeling bruised by the attitude. I was shocked by the verdict.

"My sense was that Jeff came through the five days as a griper, a complainer, an organizer of protest. He came through also as one who has for the moment at least found a kind of solace in a new religion. He became a Buddhist. I think this was a sincere conviction. I really do not believe that he believes in violence. He must have written reams and reams of protest letters. It appears to me not only from what Jeff has said but from others' testimony that Jeff must have been the most prolific complainer. Complainers in writing do not emerge as violent.

The only prosecution witness who tied Jeff directly with any of the crimes of which he was convicted was a youngster who was so visibly sick, unreliable, so obviously coached that one could not believe his testimony. This prisoner admitted that he had been told it would be good for him if he testified. He had a record of more AWOLs than time in the Army. He had a history which was not put in the record because it was not permissible. The kid was obviously mentally retarded. His memory was so faulty that you could see where he had been coached. When he was led into any other area he was in trouble. His story was so inherently incredible and he was such an unbelievable witness and there had been so much other evidence contrary to his testimony that for the court to have accepted his testimony as credible and rejected everyone else's suggests to me that no matter what standards of proof the uniform code recommends they certainly weren't applied in this case. I cannot believe that a civilian judge would not have granted a motion to dismiss or a direct verdict to end the government's case. I came away feeling that it was a travesty, that it was a preordained conviction here, a preordained sentence. It was a great shock. It is always hard to believe that people will engage in this kind of cruelty.

"I wanted to do what I could for Jeff after he was convicted. There had been a period in which his review was delayed because they did not follow the normal procedures and he was being moved from Army base to Army base and I thought this too was discriminatory and cruel treatment. They seemed to be making a political prisoner of him at that point, moving him from one place to another. I began to do what one does in these situations. I called on the Senatorial and Congressional officers who I thought might be useful. Senator Javits, Congressman Celler's office. In each case they were sympathetic and concerned but they very honestly stated that they were so flooded with this kind of problem that they didn't know where to turn. They had added staff in order to cope with the number of cases.

"In many ways Jeff was particularly unfortunate. He was almost a waif. He had no home base. He had been a Navy child which meant that he moved from base to base. He had no permanent home. I got to Lawrence Baskier. He was working with a subcommittee of the Senate and was very helpful and sympathetic.

"When the question arose of the possibility of parole for Jeff, my husband arranged employment for him when he got

out, knowing as much about Jeff as I have reported. I am suffi-
ciently convinced of the integrity and the decency of the young
man so that I had absolutely no hesitation about recommending
him for a job. This is the kind of boy we could use. Our society
is doing its best to destroy him."

To a simple lay observer the strange elements in Jeffrey's
trial started right at the beginning by the admittance of a
Colonel Emhoff to be seated as a member of the "Court" (jury)
despite the fact that the defense lawyer brought to light the
Colonel's long time friendship with Andrew Casey, the commandant of the stockade. Then came the testimony of Major
Casey himself who claimed that he had seen Terry Klug patting
people on the back. The defense objected that Terry Klug was
not on trial and that this information was therefore irrelevant.
The objection was overruled. In the end Major Casey admitted
that during the "demonstration" on June 5th he had not seen
Jeffrey Russell at all. There followed the startling testimony of
Private Allen Farrell who had been expected to be a chief government witness. He invoked his rights under Article 31 and
the Fifth Amendment of the Constitution of the United States
and proceeded to say the statement he had signed contained,
"everything they (CID) wanted me to say" and that he'd signed
the statement because he had been under severe duress. At one
point when the prosecutor, Captain Anzaldi, asked him a question he answered: "I'm sorry, sir, I can't remember what you
told me to answer to that." Though Private Farrell was threatened with perjury and could face five years if charged and
convicted, he refused to revoke any of his spoken testimony on
the stand, insisting that the CID had threatened and bribed him
into signing the statement he had signed and that he had not
seen Jeffrey Russell at any time during the riot.

Another government witness, Private William J. Miller, testified that he and Jeffrey had discussed ways of protesting the
"horrible conditions in the stockade" and both had agreed that
some effort should be made to bring these conditions to the
attention of the base officials. Miller said that Jeffrey had suggested the throwing of a footlocker out the window as a means
of dramatizing their protest but that when other prisoners discussed more violent means he and Jeffrey moved away. He also
stated: "I didn't see Russell effect any damage or violence at
all." Private Miller was used as a government witness in all of
the courts-martial and although he had been AWOL for several
weeks he was discharged without a trial.

On November 6th, the third day of the trial, the four charges of solicitation against Jeffrey were dropped, reducing his maximum sentence from fifty years to thirty years. On this same day Jeffrey testified on his own behalf. He testified that he had requested 5-10 forms to file complaints about the conditions in the stockade many times and that his complaints had had no effect; conditions in the stockade were getting worse rather than better. He also said that he had written letters to congressmen and had gotten other prisoners to write to their congressmen with no results and that in his conversation with Private Miller . . . "we considered, for instance, writing a letter to the President with a list of grievances or just drawing up a list and having everyone sign it and presenting it to Major Casey, or maybe putting it in 5-10s and requesting to see the Inspector General and presenting our case before him and things of this nature." Later on in the testimony he said: "Someone did mention let's dramatize it, throw a footlocker out the window, something to get somebody to come and listen to us." When asked if he had made this suggestion he answered: "No, I did not, definitely did not." When asked when the conversation ended he answered: "Actually it ended right after somebody suggested the footlocker."

The one witness who claimed he had seen Jeff throw a footlocker out the window was a Private Joseph Petit. On cross-examination by Judith Vladeck several inconsistencies between Petit's signed CID statement and his testimony on the stand came to light and Petit testified that the CID agent who had interrogated him had promised him immediate release from the stockade if he would sign the statement.

In the end Jeffrey Russell was convicted of arson and riot, the maximum charges against him, and despite the moving plea of Rowland Watts for leniency based on the deep need of Jeffrey's wife and baby son for Jeffrey's help, he was sentenced to three years at hard labor and a dishonorable discharge. The sentencing was delivered on a Monday after the Russells waited a harrowing weekend for the verdict. When it came, Kathy collapsed, and cried out that the Court knew beyond a shadow of a doubt that Jeffrey was innocent. She fell to the floor sobbing that she and her baby needed Jeff NOW. They had waited too long already.

After the sentencing the courtroom erupted with shouts of "Free Jeff Russell" while some people sat stunned and silent, people who could not believe that this young man had been sentenced with such a lack of hard evidence.

Russell's case did not end with the sentencing. He was abruptly sent to Fort Meade, Maryland, making it very difficult for Rowland Watts and Judith Vladeck to confer with him for a review of the case. At Fort Meade he was held in segregation he was told because of his "political beliefs." From Fort Meade he was transferred to Fort Leavenworth.

TERRY KLUG

Before the riot the conditions were unbearable in "the pound." People do not riot because they enjoy rioting. Human beings only do it because they are forced into it by unbearable circumstances. To riot is to act as animals and people only act as animals after being treated as such for a certain amount of time.

—Terry Klug

Terry's story has a happy ending. He has been fully acquitted of the riot charges and has won an appeal on a reversal of the desertion charge. He is a free man. This might be cause for rejoicing were it not for the year and a half of degrading treatment Terry received in an American stockade under an American commandant before he was declared innocent.

Terry is an appealing young man. Even in the stockade, under nightmare conditions, he maintained a real caring for his fellow prisoners. Because of his buoyant spirit, it was hard to realize how deeply he suffered from the beginning of his time in the stockade. Shortly after he received the guilty verdict and the three-year sentence from his first court-martial, for desertion, he wrote his attorney, Rowland Watts:

> I'm presently back in the "cage." My little 8-by-6 steel cell. They took all of my belongings away from me and only feed me a diet of bread, water and cold vegetables. They are back at trying to make me break again.

Terry was taken to the Fort Dix stockade on January 16, 1969. He was immediately placed in maximum security Administrative Segregation.

"I could see my clipboard outside the cell block and read 'Code 14.' I was not given any orientation. After five days, I was put in Cell Block 60 along with conscientious objectors and homosexuals. I couldn't go out without guards. . . .

"On January 28, 1969, I went to the mess hall with my fellow prisoners from Cell Block 60. A guard told us to get up after eating about five minutes. We refused. We were taken to the

Control room; it was a very cold day and we were made to stand outside for about eight hours. We were then told to return to our cell blocks. Nine or ten of us said that we wouldn't leave until we could present grievances. A guard came and told us to go to Seg. I was put in Cell Block 85. I could see the notation 'Code 5' on my clipboard. No one told me why I had been put in Seg. When Major Cashman came the next day, I asked him why I had been placed in Seg. I didn't get any answer. I contacted an ACLU lawyer, who wrote to General Collins, and I was finally released."

While Terry was out of Seg but still inside the stockade, he pleaded with his commanding officer for an outside job so that he would not have to witness the brutal behavior of guards toward other prisoners, because he did not want to go back into Seg. He could live by the letter of the law imposed on him and not respond to the cruelties meted out to him, but he knew that the harassment and beating of others could set him off—"I figured if I just stayed around the chapel during the day and buffed floors and swept and just stayed to myself, that I could handle it." He got no satisfaction from Major Casey.

Terry was in and out of Seg all his days at Dix.

"The first time I was in for four days. The second time I went, they kept me two weeks. The third time, they kept me three weeks. The next time I went I stayed there until they let me out in the middle of May. And the next time I went was after the riot and I stayed down there until I left."

Like Tom Catlow, in the months that followed the riot Terry's mail was not getting out. He never stopped complaining until finally he was taken to Major Casey's office.

"After we had gone through this whole mail scene, we talked about the riot, and I asked Major Casey why he had singled me out and the others just like that, without really having any evidence. He said that he knew it was me because it couldn't be anyone else; that I was the only Communist in Cell Block 67. He knew the type of tactics we used. He also said that he knew I was going to be convicted and that he would appear at my court-martial; he would laugh at my conviction when I burned."

Terry remembered those days with great bitterness:

"During the first few months, I was written up frequently for many different things. Sometimes I was given the reasons why I was being written up, other times I was not told. It would just be there. One time I was written up for howling like a dog. I was asleep and didn't have the slightest idea. Major Casey came by the next day and looked at my clipboard and asked me if I had been howling like a dog. I told him: 'No, I hadn't.'

"In August, perhaps September, a black prisoner named Small was brought into the cell block early in the morning when everyone was sleeping. It was about 4:00 in the morning. He was beaten by guards outside the cell block. It was around by my window. I heard them kicking him and I recognized the guards by their voices. I heard them screaming stuff like 'Kick the shit out of him. Don't let him up' and so forth and calling him names. The next day I reported this incident to Major Casey and told him that if he didn't take action, I would have to go to my civilian attorneys and we would have to bring it out to the open. He assured me that something would be done, asked me if I would make a statement to the CID. I told him I would. I was never asked to. The guards were Pfc. Marlo, Spec. 4 Frezorzi and Sergeant Mancino, the same ones that beat up Russell that first night. They were relieved of duty for 39 days and then they came back to work in the same area without any disciplinary action taken against them.

"When our civilian attorneys, Hank DiSuvero or Watts, would come down, we would meet in the correction building. The little rooms are just cubbyholes that have no roofs over them and no doors. Guards would stand next to the room and many times, I remember, the lawyers would have to get up and ask the guards to move because the conversations were supposed to be held in private. They would continually walk back and forth and look in the room."

After three days of sleeping with no mattresses and being starved, Terry and the other prisoners accused of rioting were supposed to be on A.S. food, not on "rabbit chow."

"We were supposed to receive everything on A.S. chow that is served in the mess hall, like juice, coffee, butter, salt, and we just weren't. We would have to fight for them and argue and tell Major Casey or someone who came through that we did not get any coffee. We were supposed to get coffee. It would take weeks before we would start getting coffee. We'd receive it for maybe one or two days; they would bring it down from the mess hall. Then we'd go without coffee until we complained again. We received it for another two or three days, then it would slack off again. The same with butter and juice.

"In Administrative Segregation, you are supposed to have all the privileges of anyone out in the compound. We were denied them all."

Terry Klug's mother was sixteen years old when she gave birth to him in Fort Wayne, Indiana on June 26, 1947. His father had taken off and Terry was cared for by his maternal grandmother. When Terry was five his mother married his stepfather, George Berg, in New Orleans, who worked for the State Department as an agricultural expert. Terry was brought to New Orleans to live with his mother and stepfather. He used his stepfather's name from then on until he was eighteen when he met his real father and changed his name to Klug.

Terry lived in New Orleans for about a year, at which point his stepfather started working for the FAO (Food and Agriculture Organization of the United Nations). The Bergs were sent to Nicaragua. And Terry considers that's where he "grew up." At first he lived in the country and had horses and dogs. He started in an American school with the sons of Army lifers. In the afternoons he would play with the native children. When the Bergs moved to the city of Managua itself Terry felt sad about leaving, but he grew to love the city:

"Managua was a small, dirty town, maybe two hundred thousand, maybe less, but it was a big city to me. It's the capital. I got to know the city pretty well. I drove all over with my bicycle. In Nicaragua they used to have attempted guerrilla takeovers several times a year. The guerrillas would come into the cities and there would be a curfew. The government troops would shoot anybody on the street after 6:00 P.M. Several times a year for maybe a week or two there would be battles in the streets; I didn't know what was going on. All I knew was what I heard from my parents, that people were jeopardizing our position. Every now and then I'd hear bombs going off in the city, or grenades. Then the guerrillas would leave. We lived about a block away from the presidential palace. In 1956 they shot Luis Mosa in the head several times. I was about nine. His younger son took over. I was scared by people getting shot, but I learned to grow up in that kind of atmosphere and by the time I was thirteen I was used to it.

"When I was thirteen, my parents sent me to Carlisle Military Academy, Bamburg, South Carolina. I was afraid. They had some bad, bad cats there. I got my butt beat all the time and then I started fighting back. It was only my grades that kept me in school.

"Every day I told my parents I wanted to leave, but they kind of dug it. It took everything I had not to run away. They had spent three thousand dollars to send me there.

66

"My stepfather wanted me to go back to school a second year, but I refused. So I went to El Salvador with my parents. By this time I was a sophomore in high school; I was almost fifteen. I went home to the same mess. I couldn't relate to my parents. They'd tell me to be home at eleven in the evening and I'd come in at two or three. I started drinking and hanging out in the streets. People there packed guns, so I got one too, when I was about sixteen. I was always in the streets. Sometimes I'd take off from home for two weeks; nobody knew where I was. But I kept going to school, missing a few days here and there.

"I was going to the American school. There were only 106 people in the school, so I stuck out like a sore thumb. In my second year I started hanging out with a Spanish guy who went to our school. We would swipe a car, go joyriding, and then drop it back. We started hitting the country clubs and the bars, after things were closed down, for cases of whiskey, which we'd sell for big profits. We didn't need the money; it was just something to do for excitement. The school authorities found out. My friend was expelled. He went back to the States and joined the Marines. He was killed in Vietnam not too long afterwards.

"I was put on probation. I didn't like the other kids and they didn't like me. Six weeks before the end of school, I got in a fight. They expelled me. I stayed out those six weeks and didn't try to finish my junior year anywhere, not even in a Spanish school.

"The next year my parents sent me back to the States to St. Paul's Catholic Boarding School for Boys in Covington, Louisiana, right outside of New Orleans. It was run by the Christian Brothers. It was a brand new ritzy school, but the brothers used to beat the kids up. Up to then I thought a priest was half-god, half-man. Some of those Christian Brothers had vocabularies worse than anything I'd heard in the street.

"The school was so strict that you weren't allowed to smoke until you were a senior. I was a junior when I came to school, and I'd been smoking cigarettes for two years. So I started running a cigarette ring, just enough so everyone would have some to smoke. Right before Christmas I was caught with a pack of cigarettes and they were going to expel me; they put me on double probation. So I was straight, straight. I wanted to stay there, because of my parents. I didn't want to stay there a second year, but I didn't want to go back to my parents, so I thought I'd finish off the year. I didn't have anything else to do but sit in my room and study all the time, so I made really good grades.

"In February, 1965, they let everybody in school go home for the five-day Mardi Gras holiday. Only two of us were kept back, me and a Spanish brother, Rene Lafitte. He and I could go to New Orleans during the day, but we had to be back by 12:00 every night. The next-to-the-last day Lafitte and I got back at 2:00 A.M. I walked into my room, turned on the light, and there was Brother David sitting on my bed. The next day they expelled me.

"After I was expelled, I split to my grandmother's in Indiana, and finished my junior year at public school. My grades had really dropped because I didn't do any work, but I got along well and enjoyed the people. I was going out on dates, something I hadn't done before. I'd had girlfriends and I'd been with a lot of women including prostitutes but I'd never dated like they do in the States.

"My stepfather had been transferred to Italy. I joined the family for the summer. From the moment I stepped off the plane, I really loved it. It was the end of June, right around my eighteenth birthday. My parents were cold about my getting kicked out of school and my stepfather wouldn't talk to me for days, but I started walking around the city [Rome], every day a little bit further. I'd go to a bar and have a couple of drinks. Because I spoke Spanish so well, the Italian began to make sense. I caught on very quickly. And I liked it; I liked Italy and I like the people. It was my part of the world. I recognized that right off.

"On my birthday my parents gave me a motorcycle. I could go anywhere I wanted in the city. I met Devise, an English girl whose father worked in the United Nations with my stepfather. I was her first boy friend. She was my first girl friend. Until then I had never loved anyone. I decided not to go back to the States. My parents and I had big arguments over that, but there was no way they could get me on an airplane. They didn't have too much choice, unless they wanted to kick me out completely and it hadn't gotten to that yet.

"I didn't like my parents' home. I didn't like all the big fancy things, the chandeliers. I couldn't come into the living room in my street clothes because I might get dirt or grease on the sofa. If I came home and my parents had friends in the living room, I had to change into a suit, comb my hair and shave, and come in and introduce myself. They had a nice-looking son. I'd go in there; smile, maybe have a drink with their friends, then I was supposed to shoot off to my bedroom. My friends could never go into the living room. They had to go to my bedroom.

"I spent most of the time with Devise, my girl friend. We became very close. We were both running away, trying to find ourselves. We ran into each other and took sanctuary in each other. She was rebelling in a different way. She was very quiet, and she didn't have friends. I was loud and I always had lots of friends. But we both felt the same way.

"I went to the American Overseas school in Rome, and for the first time I began to get along with my teachers.

"My favorite teacher taught English, Desmond O'Grady, an Irish poet, a beautiful, beautiful man. He was about twenty-nine and his wife twenty-six. Thanks to this teacher I caught hold of myself. He gave Devise and me the keys to his apartment. We'd go there on the weekends they were away. We had a place for ourselves where we could make love. During the week, if I wasn't getting along at home, I could stay there overnight. Desmond and I had long raps together. He'd graduated from Harvard, gone to Oxford, been everywhere and done everything. I met interesting people through him, other poets, Ezra Pound. They seemed weird to me, but I got to understand them. I loved Desmond and his wife very much. They gave me everything. There was a beautiful relationship between the four of us. We'd go dancing and drinking, together. When I could have gotten in trouble at school he rapped for me.

"I was calming down, getting my head together, beginning to understand what had been eating at me. I read a lot. I was digging Bob Dylan. Desmond and I talked about the war. I barely knew there was a war going on. This was in 1965 and 1966, and I was in Rome. Desmond was quite isolated too, being an Irish poet in Rome, but he was very liberal. He wasn't a pacifist. He just didn't believe in wars. I've always remembered him saying, 'If those bastards in Washington want to fight a war in Vietnam, let them fight a war and you just stay here.'

"My parents thought I was applying to colleges in the States, but I applied to Loyola in Rome. Anything to stay in Rome. When my parents asked me what I was going to do next year, I said: 'Well, I was just accepted at Loyola here and I think I'll be staying here.'

"They said: 'You can't. We're not paying for you to stay here and go to school. If you're going to stay here, you'll have to do it on your own.'

"I was heartbroken. I had to leave. I went back to the States. That's when I joined the Army, right after I got back to the States. Just running and running and I ran right into the Army. I did it out of anger, out of spite, out of fear. I was scared and horrified. So I hooked up with the Army.

"I had no rationalization for going into the Army. I had nothing. I just ran. I'd see signs, 'Be a man. Join the Army.' They got to me. I didn't feel any duty to fight the war. I wasn't thinking about wars at all. In fact, I joined up for Clerk-Typist School. I figured if I had a clerk-typist job, they'd have to keep me inside. The posters said 'Be a man,' and I guess I wanted to be a man. I wanted to be somebody and prove myself to other people. I still had a lot to prove. So I took them up on it.

"I joined in Indiana, and went to Fort Leonard Wood in Missouri for Basic. Basic was a choker to me. I hated everything I saw, but I kept my head. Amazingly, I didn't get into any trouble in the Army. I never even had an Article 15. But I was thinking. I figured (I'm slow, but I'm not that slow!) that you didn't have to go through that shit to be a man. I did it, but inside I was fighting back all by myself. I was like a pressure cooker. For the first time I started to explain things to myself. They made you scream 'Kill, kill, kill!' and I realized what they were doing. I was sick to my stomach.

"In the sand pits where we started doing hand-to-hand combat they had three huge posters. One was a yellow man, with slant eyes and fangs. The other had GI Joe whipping this yellow fellow. They had captions. Under one, 'Kill the enemy'; under another, 'Maim the enemy'; and under the other, 'Destroy the enemy.' I knew that they were trying to make you hate yellow people, but I didn't say anything. I kept it to myself because I was scared. I didn't know what the Army could do to you. This wasn't like school. The Army could really do a job on you. There was always the threat of the stockade. I wasn't about to go into the stockade. After Basic, I took Officers' Candidate School. So I went into Infantry, but about my seventh week I woke up one morning and said to myself: 'What the fuck am I going through all this for? What do I want to be an officer for? This is really dumb!' I went up to my best buddy and told him, 'I'm quitting. I'm doing the CO thing; I'm not doing this anymore.' He asked me to hang on for a few days to think about it, so I waited four days. My answer was the same. I told him: 'No, I can't take it. There's no reason why I should go through all this bullshit.'

"I shot off to my company officer and told him that I

wanted orders to Clerk-Typist School. I told him I didn't want to tell anybody else what to do; I didn't want to lead anybody; I didn't want to give any orders; I just wanted to be left alone. In a couple of days I had orders to Clerk-Typist School.

"That's where I ran into 'Butch,' this black dude, my brother. I met him my first day there. Butch was a real drop-out—he'd gone to college. He'd been in the stockade three times for AWOL. His talk scared me at first. I'd say: 'This guy is talking some kind of dissent.' I used to say: 'Get away from me, man, because you're going to get somebody in trouble here and it's going to be me!' But he saw that he could reach me. He kept on and on. We used to talk about the war. He hadn't been to Nam and he wasn't going to go.

"He used to ask: 'What are you going to do when you get orders?'

"I'd say: 'Man, I speak three different languages. They won't send me there.' I was trying to get to Italy. I really thought they'd send me to Europe.

"He said: 'Do you have anything against the NLF? Are they fucking up any of your friends over here? Did any of them ever call you a name? Are they bombing Washington, D.C.?' He knew what he was talking about. He knew how to reach me. After about a month and a half he'd pretty well convinced me. I wasn't going to go to war.

"At the end of training they gave him orders to Belgium. He tried everything to get out. I helped him. One time he took a whole bottle of aspirin to make them believe that he had tried to commit suicide. But he didn't get out. They kept him in Mental Hygiene for about a week. They sent him to Belgium.

"There were nineteen in my typing class. Seventeen got orders to Europe, and two got orders to Fort Bragg, North Carolina. I went to Fort Bragg. Some of those seventeen guys had wanted to stay in the States, while I had begged for Europe. It was an insult, a personal blow. It was like somebody had slapped me in the face.

"I wanted to get a leave so I could go to Europe to see Devise. When I asked them they said everybody would get a leave in a couple of months. I asked why, and they said that the company was on orders to Vietnam.

"I was shocked. I couldn't believe it.

"There were three months left before I was supposed to go to Vietnam, and I had a thirty-seven day leave. I had a hard time sleeping; sometimes I'd cry. I didn't know what to do. I went to my CO and said: 'Please take me out of the orders. Do anything, I'm not going to go. I can't go.'

"He was nice about it. He wasn't a screaming lifer. He said: 'You've got to go. Everybody in the company is going to go.'

"I pleaded with him. I told him I couldn't do it. About a week later I asked him to put me in the stockade. He said he couldn't do that because I hadn't done anything wrong. I told him: 'I'm not going to go to Vietnam. That's wrong, right?'

"He said: 'You haven't refused the order. You have to refuse an order.' I asked him to put me in there for anything. I wasn't scared of the stockade any more. He told me he couldn't do it! 'You just go on your leave and I'm sure you'll decide that the best thing to do is to go over there with the rest of the men.'

"I told him: 'I know that if I go on that leave, I won't come back.' I used to go to him every couple of days and tell him: 'I haven't changed my mind. I'm all screwed up. You've got to do something. If I go on that leave, I'm not coming back.' He said: 'Yes, you will.' So I took my leave, went to Europe, and didn't come back.

"I stayed in Rome for five months. I told my parents I was going back to the States. Instead I started living in an apartment in downtown Rome with Devise. I worked in a movie and made a little money. I never bumped into my parents though I saw them drive past a few times.

"After five months I started running short of money and began to worry that somebody would turn me in; I could have been extradited from Italy. So I shot up to France; I'd read that they couldn't extradite you from France. I told Devise to sit tight. (She was going to go to art school in England by this time.) I'd go to France; she'd go to England and go to school and that as soon as I had everything square I'd send for her. I went to Paris, and started looking for people. I finally ran into Max [an American political worker], and Max introduced me to Dick Perrin. We started working together.

"Then Devise wrote that she wasn't coming to Paris. That blew my mind for about three weeks. I went wild, got into fights and really fucked up some bars—glasses, trays, people and everything. Finally I got beaten up badly. I thought every bone in my body was broken.

"I went to Antibes to recuperate. I worked in a flower shop and started reading a lot. It was quiet and I had a lot of time to myself. I lived with an older woman. She was thirty-five and I was twenty. I met young leftist students with her. I started working with CVN [Comité Vietnam Nationale] and with another committee which was connected with JCR [Jeunesses Communistes Révolutionnaires] Young Revolutionary Communists. They were the leading student groups in the May and June uprising in Paris. I went to meetings, wrote a couple of articles, gave a couple of speeches, I read anything political I could get my hands on—Trotsky, Lenin, Mao, Guevara.

"I was still connected with Perrin and Max in Paris. We found that a few GIs wanted to do something as GIs in France. They started a newsletter, *The Act*, in Paris. I wrote an article for it. RITA [Resistance Inside the Army] had just been formed in Paris. They did a television show on it. This was about February 12, 1968. I kept in touch with them all the time by phone. They called me back for an international press conference.

"I stayed in Paris about two weeks. Then I shot back to the Riviera. In March I went back to Paris. Dick and I started living together. We worked, spoke, and wrote. I had a few squibs in newspapers in the U.S. I had a two-page article in the *Overseas Weekly*. I spoke at several universities.

"May-June was the first time I'd had a chance to see any action—everything else had just been words, reading and meetings. It was a beautiful experience.

"After the uprising was smashed there was a witch hunt, and I had to leave the country. I went to Switzerland. I made a few speeches, did a few interviews, a few filmings. People were interested because I had just come from Paris. They had a three-day student revolt there and I got involved in that. I got front page pictures. When I got back to Paris they were mad at me because I was supposed to be quiet, taking a rest.

"In Paris, Dick and I shared the same place. We did a lot of talking, went to meetings all the time; really ran ourselves down. We progressed together. We worked all the time; read together, wrote together. Dick was a very good man. He worked with Andy Stapp at Fort Sill in the early days. Dick and I both joined the Union (American Servicemen's Union) right after it was formed. We started RITA as a chapter of the Union in Europe.

"Then Dick and I began to feel that we'd accomplished what we could in Europe, which really wasn't very much. We both felt guilty about advocating what we were advocating but not personally suffering the consequences. They couldn't touch me in Paris. I'd been thinking about going back since April.

In September I made up my mind. It took me months, because I didn't want to go to jail. But that was my decision and I stood by it.

"I wanted to organize within the Army. I just couldn't see being AWOL and advocating Army organizing. I wasn't trying to punish myself by going to jail. In fact, when I went to jail, I tried for months to get back to duty. I told them: 'Give me time if you want to, but don't discharge me. Send me back to duty.' Dick and I turned ourselves in in Paris. They sent someone from the Pentagon to talk to us. The Pentagon guy wanted information, names of people. We told him no. We were honest; we told him why we wanted to go back. He said: 'You're crazy!' So he shot back to the Pentagon and left us sitting there. I had orders to go to Fort Bragg—military orders cut in the Embassy by the Military Attaché, and I really thought I was going to Fort Bragg. I didn't know what I'd be facing if I went back. I thought: 'Just get me back there and I'll see what's going on and get a lawyer and maybe we can work something out.' I felt I'd be more effective in the States than sitting around in Europe. Dick decided against it. He left the day before I did, for Canada. I left January 16 for New York."

On October 20, 1969, almost five months after Terry had been smuggled back into Seg accused of riot charges, he received his pretrial Article 39A hearing. Terry's civilian defense attorney, Henry DiSuvero, then of the Emergency Civil Liberties Committee, filed twenty-two motions on Terry's behalf.

A motion for trial by jury of his peers as required under Article III of the U.S. Constitution and the Fifth and Sixth Amendments was denied.

A motion to dismiss all charges on the grounds that they were returned in violation of the defendant's First Amendment rights was denied. This referred to the fact that the Criminal Investigation Division had illegally seized some of Terry's papers. On this motion the Court ruled that the defense would be able to resubmit the motion and the further motions to suppress the evidence, if the trial counsel entered the paper into evidence at Terry's court-martial.

A motion to dismiss on grounds of unlawful use of command influence was denied. Article 22 of the Uniform Code of Military Justice states that it is unlawful for the accuser to convene a general court-martial against the accused. General Collins, Commander of Fort Dix, was the convening authority at this trial (the person ordering the court-martial). Defense attorney DiSuvero presented evidence that General Collins had met with the Criminal Investigation Division and had authorized the CID to offer "considerations" in return for statements from prisoners. Later the Commander of the First Infantry upheld the General's decision and the Court agreed to allow the defense to reopen on this motion.

Motions to dismiss charges against Terry because of prior punishment and failure to provide Terry with a speedy trial were denied. The Court would not hear testimony as to the conditions under which Terry was held in punitive confinement since June 6th.

Other motions to dismiss based on a lack of evidence introduced by the government were denied.

A motion to drop the charge of conspiracy against Terry was granted based on multiplicity of evidence in bringing the additional charge of riot.

At the end of his 39A hearing, Terry was faced with general court-martial charges of a possible maximum sentence of thirty years, ten for the riot charge and twenty for aggravated arson.

Terry's court-martial stemming from the riot charges was highly dramatic not only because his was the one *acquittal* of the five, but because three Dostoevskian characters were flushed into the courtroom. Under examination and cross-examination, these three revealed further stockade horrors. There was the victim, the oppressor, and the quisling. The victim, Private Willie McCartha, was so pitiable that it is difficult to understand why the Army had not discharged him on medical grounds long before. The oppressor, Major Andrew Michael Casey, with his relentless personal spite for Terry Klug, gave unashamed testimony to an arrogance equal to any stockade commander Hollywood dreams up for enemy prison camps. The quisling, Captain Ross Anzaldi (who had been Terry's Army defense lawyer in his desertion court-martial), ironically, was instrumental in gaining an acquittal for Terry.

The first deposition in the Klug trial was by a government witness, Private William James McCartha, a tall thin black man with deep-set eyes and a delicate, almost feminine face. He stood over six feet tall, normally weighed 190 pounds, but he had lost over twenty pounds in the stockade. The deposition had to be adjourned abruptly several times because of his sickness. McCartha claimed that Terry Klug, Jeffrey Russell and William Brakefield had approached him in the mess hall at lunch on June 5th and told him there was to be some activity at 8:00 P.M. that evening. When asked by the defense counsel if after his dishonorable discharge (which he was to receive in five days), he expected to live in the New York area, his reply was: "I hope so, if I'm not dead."

While reading Defense Exhibit A, which defense attorney DiSuvero had given him to read, McCartha asked to speak to his counsel and over the objections of defense counsel, the witness suddenly left the stand and crossed the room, and spoke privately with Captain Olsen (the trial counsel) who was seated in the spectator section of the room. After further objections and discussions, it evolved that McCartha had asked his counsel: "If he could get my pills and what-not because I felt like I was going to pass out." The document he had been reading referred to his mental strain at the time the CID had taken his statement.

On further cross-examination, it developed that McCartha had been on bed rest June 5th on doctor's orders because in his own words, "I had a nervous breakdown that day . . . I started shaking. My mouth freezed up, like it froze my muscles in my jaw. I can't hardly breathe and I can't think right . . . I get dizzy and feel like I'm going to pass out." Nevertheless he had gone for lunch, and had thrown up his lunch. Further cross-examination revealed that James McCartha's real name was William James McCarthur, that guards had written many papers for him asking for a medical discharge and that he had signed them without reading them. His history was so pathetic that although he was a government witness, his story actually incriminated the Army and the stockade for treating a very sick man as a criminal rather than as a patient.

McCartha stated: "Ever since I took Basic I took a nervous condition but it wasn't that bad. It really got bad this year." When asked, "And being in Segregation, did that aggravate your nervous condition?" his pitiful answer was: "Yes, being closed up. I have ever since I was small a record of claustrophobia . . . you're in a cell all day long except for fifteen minutes. It depends if you're doing DS or AS. AS is regular chow." McCartha had been on DS, but he denied that it aggravated his nervous condition because: "I couldn't eat anything anyway. Maybe sometimes I could drink a glass of water or put down a piece of bread."

During further cross-examination, McCartha revealed that he'd had two nervous attacks in Segregation, "but one time they put me in straps. Another time they put me in the hospital."

After hospitalization, they had given him sixty milligrams of Librium every two hours. DiSuvero then asked if he had had this dosage June 5th. McCartha said no. DiSuvero asked: "You were on it that day?"

McCartha said: "No, they doubled it that day . . . they hit me with twenty-five cubic centimeters of the Thorazine and twenty-five milligrams of Librium."

DiSuvero said: "When you went up to the CID and gave him your statement, do you recall any conversation you had with the CID agent?"

McCartha answered: "No, not right now. I told you I was in a very upset mood at that time and I was shaking like a leaf. They took me to the hospital when I was talking to them because I got very upset and started shaking and they took me to the hospital and brought me back."

On further examination, it evolved that Captain Anzaldi had held several interviews with McCartha and that at one of those interviews, his counsel, Captain Olsen, had not been present.

Early in September, 1970, after all the trials were over and four of the five young men were doing their time at Fort Leavenworth, Terry included—though he had received an acquittal on the riot charge, his desertion charge had yet to be reversed —Henry DiSuvero spoke about Terry Klug's trial in relation to the other Fort Dix court-martial riot trials and in the perspective of military justice:

"In a way going to a court-martial is very much like going to practice in a very small Southern town. The entire power structure is white, very straight, and concerned with order and discipline. It's very resentful of outsiders coming in. It's very prideful of the nominal lip service that's paid to the forms of justice rather than the substance of it and it's very, very intolerant of any threat to that structure, and so what you have is a classic situation. The machinery makes a great pretense of due process while denying the substance of it to the people who do challenge the structure. In some ways the closeness of it all appalled me.

"Practicing in a regular criminal court there is a certain élan that exists among defense lawyers, and they do not see their roles as interchangeable with prosecutors. There's a certain distance that exists between them as well as between them and the judge. That distance simply does not exist in the military situation. Usually what happens is that a beginning lawyer in the JAG office starts on the defense side, and as he gets better he gets transferred to the prosecution side, and if he stays for any length of time he's sent to military judge school; so although there's a normal respect given to the fact that everyone has experience on both sides of the street, there's no built-in avid defense that's provided. No other criminal court really works that way. The other aspect that differs from a civilian court is that the major assumption that exists in military courts is that it's a disciplinary agency and that's built in by the kind of court [jury] that they have. It almost always has to be a body of officers who are superior to the person who is caught. The defendant has no chance of appearing before a jury of his peers. However, having said all of this, I felt that there was at times a deliberate leaning over backwards in showing or trying to show that there was a sense of fairness in the operation of the military justice system.

"I feel very ambiguously about Judge Nichols [Judge Nichols presided at all the courts-martial at Fort Dix]. I think in the Klug trial, Nichols was punctilious in making sure that he would not be reversed by acceding in almost every instance to practically every defense motion we made. I think that in part he anticipated that the evidence would be so strong that nevertheless Klug would be convicted. You see what a judge does, I mean my view of a judge, is that he is primarily concerned about being reversed on appeal. The tactics of defense lawyers is to try and exclude evidence that the prosecution might have to enter against the defendant by making a series of motions to gain that result. The judge then has to decide whether he's going to exclude or not exclude that evidence. If he makes a mistake and lets the evidence in, that conviction may be reversed; if he keeps the evidence out that's not a basis for reversal. My feeling is that what Nichols was doing was acceding to our request to keep evidence out, anticipating that there would still be a conviction and that there would be no basis for a reversal.

"In all of these cases Captain Ross Anzaldi plays a very strange role. It was fortuitous that Anzaldi had previously been a defense counsel for Klug. It was fortuitous in that we came up with a novel argument. The argument was essentially that since Anzaldi had been a defense counsel for Klug, a lawyer-client relationship had been established between them, and although he was involved in the prosecution side in another riot case, he could not in any way help convict his former client. He did not prosecute in our case. What he had done was to help develop information which was used by our prosecutor and that was enough for Nichols to exclude that person from the witness stand. The two big pieces of evidence that he kept out of the Klug trial were the testimony of the witness Miller, and that was because of Anzaldi, and the other was the testimony of Farrell and that was also because of Anzaldi.

"In the Klug case the only witness who presented testimony of an incriminating nature was the one witness, McCartha, and I think we fairly discredited him. Also the stockade Commander, Major Casey, said that he had seen Klug congratulating people after the incident. The testimony of Major Casey, I think, was fairly discredited by cross-examination. He was shown to be a very hostile person whose hostility was directed against this defendant.

"I think Casey is a very clever person who is hard as a stockade commander. I think he comes out of an old school of authoritarian thinking. Casey is on the short side and has a pugnacious bearing about him. He's very cordial to those whom he feels are his equals. There's no doubt that he feels a man's worth is measured by his rank and that clearly was exhibited throughout the management of the stockade. I think he was terribly embarrassed and possibly had his career set back as a result of the stockade corruption. His streak of sadism came out in the Klug trial. One of the questions that we asked him was: Was it a fact that he had said to Klug, 'I'm going to come to your trial and I'm going to laugh and laugh and laugh'? That was my last question in cross-examination and he had to answer yes."

JAIL CO TESTIFIES HE "NEVER LIKED" KLUG

By James E. Humes, Staff Writer

FORT DIX—The assistant stockade commander here has testified that he "never particularly liked" Pvt. Terry Klug, whose general court-martial for involvement in a June 5 post stockade riot entered its second day today.

Major Andrew Casey, who was stockade commander at the time of the riot, admitted his dislike under cross-examination yesterday.

"Didn't you say once, 'Klug, I'm going to your trial and I am going to laugh and laugh'?" asked Henry DiSuvero, Klug's civilian lawyer.

"No doubt I said words to that effect," Casey replied evenly.

"You cannot name any other person you disliked

with the same intensity as you did Klug in Cell Block 67?" DiSuvero of the National Emergency Civil Liberties Committee also asked.

"No, I didn't know any others as well as Klug," the assistant stockade commander replied . . .*

* *The Evening Times*, Trenton, N.J., December 2, 1969.

THOMAS CATLOW

I am one of the Fort Dix thirty-eight. I am only seventeen. My name is Thomas Catlow. I am facing forty years for the June 5th revolt at the stockade. . . .

The Army would like to know why there actually was a revolt at the Fort Dix stockade on the evening of June 5th. It's simple! You can deprive men of their essential manhood and treat them like animals for so long until they finally stand up and fight back . . .

. . . If the American people really believe men should be jailed for going home or refusing to kill in a war that we do not have any interest in, please send me to another country. I would rather go to jail than be forced to murder Vietnamese people in a needless war.

What has become of our sense of reasoning?

> **—Excerpts from a statement by
> Thomas Catlow in *Shakedown*,
> October 17, 1969**

Tom Catlow is a freckle-faced redhead with the gift of gab, quick temper and the free and easy manner that would conjure up pure undistilled Irish parentage. Actually only his maternal grandfather came from Irish stock. His maternal grandmother was a French-Canadian Indian. Tom's father's family came here from England.

Tom opposed the service to begin with. He makes no bones about it: "I didn't believe in the war and the only reason I enlisted was to get out of jail, not to be a soldier."

Tom was railroaded into the Army the way many young men have been and still are. A juvenile court judge presented him with the alternative of three years in the Army or doing an indefinite five in jail. Coerced enlistment goes against military laws and from the point of view of civil law this choice of Army or jail constitutes a sentencing without trial. However, this illegal Army or jail sentencing continued unabated in America throughout the period of the Vietnam war. Tom had no legal counsel. He signed preliminary enlistment papers when he was sixteen. On his seventeenth birthday he was released from jail and completed signing the papers. Tom Catlow arrived at Fort Dix on November 20, 1968.

Tom was born in Jersey City, November 14, 1951. His mother was a housekeeper and his father a bartender. His parents separated when he was three years old. He lived with his mother until at the age of five he broke a plate glass window and his mother felt he was too much for her and sent him packing to his father, a heavy drinker. His mother took him back after the summer and he was well-behaved until he was thirteen or fourteen when he got into a fight with a teacher at Keyport High School in Monmouth, New Jersey and was expelled from school. He fought with his mother and he left home. His mother had him arrested and he spent thirty days in a detention home in Freehold, New Jersey. He went to court, got out of the detention home and moved in with his aunt in Freehold. Both Tom's parents have been married several times and he has a great array of brothers, sisters, and step-siblings. Tom was the only one of the children that his father fought for and after a couple of months of staying with his aunt, his father came for him. He completed the ninth grade at Weehauken High School and was starting the tenth when he got into a fight with his father, moved out of that home, quit school and was arrested and put into Secaucus Youth Center. From there he was taken to the Monmouth County Jail, and given the option of a long jail sentence or three years in the Army. Tom had a big list of petty thefts and burglaries against him, some of which he was responsible for and some not. He chose the Army. His mother signed the papers.

Tom completed Basic Training at Fort Dix and started Advance Individual Training at a wire man school. He was halfway through the eight-week course when he was taken and put on holdover awaiting a court-martial for an hour and forty-five minutes AWOL, aggravated assault and illegal use of prescription drugs. He was put on restriction. He left, went AWOL again, but turned himself in twenty-nine days later. He was put in the stockade at Fort Dix, court-martialed in April, 1969, for two counts of AWOL, disrespect to a commissioned officer and disobeying a lawful order. He got six months in the stockade. On May 5, 1969, he escaped from the stockade. He was apprehended seven days later; while he was being brought back to the stockade he escaped again, was apprehended again the same day. On June 3rd he had his second court-martial, was reconvicted for AWOL and sentenced to three months additional confinement in the stockade. In all, he had nine months ahead of him, plus a seventy-five-dollar fine added to previous fines. Once in the stockade all pay is deducted automatically and Tom was penniless to begin with.

Tom remembered his days in Segregation as ones of continual harassment and cruelty and Tom had hardly come from a protected background:

"The first time I went to Seg I was down there for escape and the night I went down what happened was they didn't know that I had escaped and that I was down there for escaping. I would have been put in a Seg cell had they known but when they called up from Control that the duty officer needed a mattress, a pillow and a pillow case so he could sleep, I was picked to help the guards bring the stuff up there and while I was up there one of the guards asked me if I hadn't been in the stockade before and I said, yes, I had, only a few days before. He asked me how I had gotten out and I said I had escaped so then they told me I was going down to Seg. When I got down to Seg there weren't any beds there either, so they decided I should go to Cell Block 85 but there weren't any beds there either, so they sent me to Cell Block 60, out of Segregation to get a bunk. They made me run with it. It was a metal bunk. When I got it to 85 they told me it was the wrong bunk and I had to bring it back again and I had to run back with it and bring another one. After I ran back with the other one, brought it in to the cell, made it up, they decided they were going to move the clean-up man out of his cell and I was to move into his cell.

"I seen a lot of things. I seen a lot of guys slit their wrists. And I seen one guy, Michael Pena slit his throat with a razor blade. They took him to the hospital and sewed stitches in his throat and brought him back to his cell. Michael Pena was a special case, but lots of guys did it because they couldn't take being locked up. It was the first time they were in jail and they were like twenty-five or twenty-six years old and they had never been arrested before in their lives. They had no police record whatsoever. They had enlisted in the service and they were in the stockade because they went home to help their families out or they didn't want to go to Vietnam. They'd be put in Seg and the harassment was just too much for them. It's just that it piles up and piles up, the screaming at you constantly, about sixteen hours a day and having to sit in your cell for sixteen hours a day with nothing to read. The cell is six by eight by nine feet, I think, and it's all green inside and there's either a mesh cell or a regular cell. A regular cell is just a little cell with bars in front with a commode and a steel bunk which is two and a half feet off the ground and is held up by chains. A mesh cell, the bars are covered by a mesh screen so that you can't pass anything in or out. Those are in Cell Block 71 where there are seven of them and seven regular cells where the bunks are wooden bunks six inches off the ground. In the mesh cells you have a light in the ceiling with a screening over it so that you can't take the bulb out. In the other cells you have no light. You're supposed to get enough illumination from the lights down the hall. No windows. The commode or toilet have no seats on them. They're push buttons, no sinks.

"You're in your cell all day except for exercise. If you're an A.S. [Administrative Segregation] prisoner you're out for an hour and if you're a D.S. [Disciplinary Segregation] prisoner you're out of your cell for fifteen minutes. A.S., you're in there for escaping or because you're a homosexual or you're under investigation; a D.S. prisoner means that you're under discipline for some action that the Commander of the stockade has decided is wrong. The only other time that you're out of your cell except to exercise is to shower and shave at night. In Seg you're woken up at 5:00 in the morning, you have to stockade your mattress and bunk and you sit down and wait and your breakfast comes to you, any time from 5:30 to 7:30 and they bring you a tray with your food on it and after you're finished you slide it under the door. After you finish breakfast you sit down and read. If you're a D.S. prisoner the only material you're allowed to read is religious material, like the Bible, or religious newspapers or some things you get after chapel, Catholic or Protestant. If you were a Muslim you weren't allowed to have books on the Muslim religion; Buddhist, the same. And if you're Jewish you are usually told to have your family mail material to you because they would say: 'We don't have *that* material here.' All day long in Seg you sit there, day after day after day. The first time I was there for fifteen days and the second time I was there for about seven months.

"While we were in Seg it was summer and it got to be winter time. The shower room was in the front of the cell block. Usually the doors to the cell block are open because the guards run in and out. When you take a shower you may be ten feet from the door. When you get out of the shower you're wet. If you get a hot shower it doesn't mean anything, because cold air is coming in and it's going to be cold. Only the first three people ever got hot showers anyway. After that the hot water ran out. Only the halls were heated and Major Casey decided they should never go over 70 degrees. Most of them shut off and wouldn't go back on again until it got to be 60 or 55 degrees. Anyway if it was 60 or 70 in the hallway outside your cell, it was 50 or 60 inside. The hot air did not stay in those cells. They stayed cold; they were steel, completely steel cells. Then there was a month of no heat.

"I had a few things happen to me. On July 27th or 28th George Caputo was court-martialed at Special Courts for calling an officer a 'fucker.' I went to his trial; so did Terry Klug, Bill Brakefield, Jeff Russell, Allan Farrel. We went up there as character witnesses; others too, Ronnie Krupp and others, a few of them as regular witnesses who had seen what happened. While we were there, before we went in, George got into an argument with an E5, a sergeant. We were in the bull pen. I went over to George and I said: 'George, cool it; because you're not going to get anywhere with him because you see he's outside and you're inside. That means he's the boss and he's the big man as long as he's outside the fence; but once he comes inside here he's not going to say anything because there's too many of us.' The Sergeant didn't like what I said and so he took me out of the bull pen. They're all considered bull pens where you just sit and wait. Some of them are fenced-in rooms and some are just rooms with steel bars for doors and steel bars on the windows.

"Anyway I was taken into a little room across from the bull pen and handcuffed to a chair and another sergeant, not the one that George had been arguing with, came in and he smacked me and he punched me a few times and he stood there and screamed at me as he smacked me, and told me I would have to go into the bull pen with him and this other sergeant and apologize and if he didn't like my apology he would take me back again and kick my ass. Seeing as how I was handcuffed to a chair and I couldn't fight back I decided the best thing I should do was apologize, so I told him I would. We went in and I apologized in front of everyone to the Sergeant for saying what I had said and the other sergeant said:

SERGEANT: I don't like the way you apologized.

[We walked out of the bull pen.]

CATLOW: I'm not going into that room again because I'm not going to let you handcuff me to that

85

chair and kick the shit out of me. I'm not stupid.

[He grabbed me.]

SERGEANT: Get into that room over there and I'm not going to do anything. What are you trying to start trouble for?

CATLOW: I'm not going in there with you.

SERGEANT: The only reason I want to take you in there is to talk to you. I want to question you.

CATLOW: If you want to question me call my military lawyer up. He's up at the JAG office and if you're going to question me I want him here.

SERGEANT: No.

[And he pushed me.]

"I was across from the bull pen against the wall and I started to move out of the way and he hit me in the chest and knocked me into a coffee table and knocked the coffee pot over and someone ran into the courtroom and Lonnie Levy [then of the Emergency Civil Liberties Committee] came out and other people and while she was arguing with the Sergeant who had hit me the other Sergeant handcuffed me and took me into the room and handcuffed me to the chair. After she went back into the courtroom, he came back and did a number on me while I was handcuffed, and as they were taking me out of the room my military lawyer, Captain Furr, came up because they had called him and he took me into another room. There were hand prints on my face. Captain Furr made a big stink about it and took statements from people. In the end the commander of SPD [holding facility. See "Afterword: The Cage."] said he looked into the matter and there was no reason for anyone to be disciplined.

"I seen a number of people being beaten up. I seen some people being put in straps—one guy was Paul Tanski. He was put in straps for about sixteen, seventeen hours. Straps are leather straps that you wear like handcuffs and your hands are tied to your ankles behind. You're like in a half circle on your stomach. He stayed in them all night.

"I was smacked around one night for making my bunk too early. Sergeant Chitwood did it—when they came down and I had made my bunk early, he knocked me in the corner of

86

the cell and he smacked me around and these two guards held me while he smacked me. I reported it. Captain McClendon supposedly made an investigation. Two days later Captain McClendon called me up and said: 'Look, I don't want you to do anything about this. I talked it over and I found out that Sergeant Chitwood was in the wrong, and I spoke to him, and it won't happen again so you don't have to do anything about it.' That's as far as it went. Nobody could do anything.

"People were knocked around all the time. One incident was with Robert Small who was beat up outside Cell Block 85. The guards that did it were three guards, E5 Mancino and Pfc. Fiseyse and Pfc. Marlo [sic]. They were relieved of duty for 40 days [sic] and put under investigation and they decided that they hadn't done anything wrong. When they came back from their 40-day leave, Marlo and Fiseyse were both Spec. 4. They had advanced a rank for beating up this prisoner. The week they came back was the week of one of the trials. I believe it was Farrel's trial and they were assigned to take us to the trial every day so they didn't work in Seg. But the first night they worked, after being relieved of duty for 40 days, they beat up three different prisoners who were brought in that night. Outside where the prisoners were handcuffed, they worked them over, these same guards who had just come back from being relieved of duty.

"I was outside my cell when they started to knock Stanley Goldstein around. I was put in my cell and I could hear him screaming for help . . . I seen them start to hit him. They told Stanley if he got a lawyer or reported it in any way or asked to see mental or physical hygiene, that they would take away his honorable discharge, he wouldn't get the GI bill and he would be given another court-martial for insubordination or some kind of thing. Stanley was in on a trumped-up AWOL for which he was convicted. He was scheduled for release from the stockade in 40 days. He was going to get out of the Army and it was pending . . . it was hanging in the air whether they would give him an honorable discharge or dishonorable. He had been accepted to go to school on the GI bill which the Army knew about—the stockade knew about—the only thing was he had to be released with an honorable discharge. So what they told Stanley was if he reported the incident in any way or if he tried to get any medical help, because he was pretty badly beaten up, forget it. Stanley did not get a lawyer, he did not report it and he got no help whatsoever. It was a whole thing and for two weeks his wife and sister thought he was really sick. They thought he was injured internally because he was just in a daze. What the guards had said was, you know, we beat you up and if you tell on us we're going to see to it that you're not going to school and you get court-martialed so that incident went unrecorded.

"There was this guy, Charlie, who comes from Jersey City. The day he came into the stockade, he was tripping. He was stoned out on acid and speed. They took him to the hospital and admitted him as a deaf and dumb mute, which was really weird. After he came off his trip and he was considered well, they brought him back to the stockade. He was no longer a deaf and dumb mute. He did about a month or two in Seg. Then he had a violent flashback from acid. He's an acid head. He really got into it while he was in Vietnam and he beat up a sergeant in C Compound and they brought him down to Seg. And they strapped him up to put him on a stretcher, he broke the straps. And they didn't know what to do so they put ten or twenty straps over him and got him to the hospital. They give you one shot of Thorazine to knock you out if you've had a bad flashback. They gave him one shot and it didn't work. So they gave him another one. It didn't work, and they they gave him another one and it knocked him out and they brought him back. But the total of all this—the three shots of Thorazine would be considered an overdose . . . and they gave him an overdose of Thorazine and the thing is, to combat acid, you do not use Thorazine. It's been coming out now that you can't use Thorazine to combat acid because it really messes up your brain waves and brain cells. For about a month after this he sat in his cell and did nothing at all. He had this fear of everything. And when anyone opened up the cell door in his cell he would jump up and quiver in the corner and scream and cry and everything and he finally, slowly, came out of it. And he went to his trial and he had a special court-martial for nine months AWOL and he went over his record in the stockade and he was found not guilty. And he got released and he got a discharge and everything. He went to a mental hospital from what I understand. But he wasn't very straight anyway because while he was in Vietnam, him and his buddy were involved in one of those little massacres. Him and four other guys—captured a Vietnamese girl, raped her, and then he slit her throat."

Thomas Catlow's court-martial was the second of the five in connection with the June 5th stockade riot. It was the only one in which the defendant and the civilian lawyer parted on less than friendly terms. Tom's civilian counsel was Fred Cohn, a member of the "Law Commune," a group of young politically oriented lawyers.

Fred is a maverick. All the other civilian lawyers who worked on cases at Fort Dix were fairly conservatively dressed. They looked like they might be lawyers. Fred was something else. He has a huge swarthy head, not unlike a blown-up cartoon of Stalin, with a great mass of jet-black unruly hair and a thick, black, drooping moustache. He sported wild large ties and unconventional clothes in court. The expression on the faces of JAG officers when they first saw Fred was always worth watching. A look came over them of such total astonishment that watching them made one wonder what eighth wonder of the world they were witnessing. The whole military freeze was shattered and they looked out like little boys.

After the initial shock, the JAG officers seemed particularly eager to help Fred. He has a great verbal sense of humor and an unstifled sense of liveliness. Still he was not insensitive to the fact that Tom did not agree with his tactics in handling Tom's defense. Fred reminisced on the case one day in September, 1970:

"I had tried a number of the Fort Hood 43 in Filene, Texas and I had done other military stuff for the National Lawyers Guild, Military Law Practice at the time before it was associated with the ECLC. When I went down to Fort Dix, I went for them. I was doing all this as a cooperating lawyer. I was in private practice. I was not paid by them. I would take time out from my practice to do these political kind of cases. I now belong to what is called by most people in the Movement, the 'Law Commune' though we don't use that name. We use the names of the people who work there, all the lawyers' names. I've always felt that lawyers who work for military-political organizers are very important to the movement, essentially because if you're going to organize the working class around political issues today, it's very difficult to do, as we've seen down at Wall Street [the hardhat demonstration]; but when you get to people while they're in the Army, they have a more basic understanding of the issues because they're being more oppressed. It's a visible kind of oppression. Viscerally, I felt this two or two and a half years ago, but I don't think I made the rational analysis until recently.

"I represented Catlow. First of all Catlow had confessed and when I got into the picture he had recanted on his confession. Another thing was that Catlow was very, very young. I must say that in all honesty Catlow and I parted with the feelings that our dealings together had not been a great success and that's one of the problems in dealing with political cases. I thought that legally it was a great success, well at least partly. He should have been found not guilty, but having been found guilty he didn't get any appreciable sentence. And a dishonorable discharge today in some circles is a badge of honor, but there were problems in the political handling of the case which is always a problem that political lawyers have to be aware of. I did want a joint trial in this case and I was overruled by the other attorneys and their clients, but the essential political problem that I ran into was that I called the stockade Commander [Major Casey] as a witness in mitigation for Tom Catlow and as a direct result of that Tom got no time in jail. There was a lot of feeling by a lot of people that since the riot had been against the stockade you shouldn't use the stockade Commander, the enemy, on your side—but you're faced with a couple of dilemmas: one is protecting your client to the utmost and making a political judgment as to whether or not doing such a thing is damaging politically. In that particular circumstance, at least in retrospect, Tom does feel it was damaging. But I felt there were other political points to be made, to bring to light that one of the ways that the Army recruits people is using the Army as a punishment.

"Tom got into the Army out of jail. He was given his choice of either go to jail or go into the Army. I thought it was good, politically, for the Commander of the stockade to say that this is a terrible way to recruit people into the Army. He did and he said that jail's not going to serve this kid any good. He's going to be a bad soldier no matter what you do. Why don't you just send him home . . . Major Casey said that. There are all sorts of reasons that he said it, some of which were good and some of which were bad but as long as we could get him to say it, I felt that was fine. There are always differences in judgments, given hindsight.

"There are errors made by all sorts of people and I am not about to ascribe blame to anyone, whether it was mine or whether it was Tom's or anybody else's. Terry Klug was acquitted partly because of Anzaldi but partly because Hank DiSuvero tried a great case. Essentially the reason why Klug got acquitted was because he didn't do it, but then it's true neither did Russell or Brakefield or Rodriguez or Catlow. And what was intriguing—what seemed to be apparent in Catlow's case, what many of us who have tried a number of military cases know—is that the court-martial board will convict and then resolve reasonable doubt in the sentence: 'Well, there's a small chance that he might not be guilty, even from our perspective, we'll tell you what we'll do: let's convict him and then we'll let him off. We've got that power.' I think they do that quite often and I think that's what they did in Tom's case. We mounted an attack on the confession which I thought was quite successful.

"We showed under cross-examination of the government's own witnesses that soldiers had been bribed for confessions, had gotten all sorts of promises, had been threatened, had never read the confessions they signed. We had one soldier faced with a conflicting statement that he had made earlier. He said: 'Well I never said what was in that confession. I mean, they just put that in front of me and I just signed it. They told me to sign it and I did.'

"Another one said he had never read the confession, in fact he was illiterate [Petit]. He was a functional illiterate. I don't think he could read any word more than one syllable. Another interesting thing was I managed to disqualify in my court-martial procedure two successive presidents of the Court-Martial Board—I believed they were antithetical to the interests of my client—by the use of the Army's own procedure, which I think is a horrid procedure.

"When somebody is up for court-martial the first step in the procedure is an Article 32 proceeding. The case is referred [by an officer to an officer] first of all. Then the Article 32 officer takes evidence and rules on it, makes a recommendation on it. Then it goes to the JAG office where the Judge Advocate makes a recommendation. Finally it goes to the convening authority who in this case is the general. Supposedly each of these people takes a look at the evidence and asks is there enough evidence to send this man to a general court-martial. Well if you question a line officer who has some court-martial convening jurisdiction, who knows the chain of command it goes through, if you question him it becomes apparent that this whole procedure reduces the presumption of innocence because they know that, if you take a position, if you ask a colonel do you think it's a serious matter to send somebody for a court-martial he will of course say yes. They'll say of course it's a serious matter. They wouldn't do it unless they thought there was a lot of evidence in the case and obviously if the general had done it they must feel that the soldier in question is pretty well guilty so the fact comes out that there's a presumption of guilt not innocence.

"I managed to deal with two colonels, one lieutenant colonel and one full colonel in a very peremptory manner and got them the hell off the board and wound up with the President of the Board who was a social worker who had never referred anybody to any court-martial in eighteen years, at which point I stopped and said go ahead. True that in case of another court they left a friend of Casey's on the court [Russell's].

"Colonel Nichols, the judge in all the cases, was not the most dispassionate of men and subject to some pressures of his own I suppose. You could make an intriguing analysis of military judges, the way they view themselves. They're not essentially courageous souls. Most of them have an eye to their pensions and where they want to do their duty. Colonel Nichols is very nice. He floats into the office at around 10:00 every day in his nice white sport jacket and he's very cute, a very pleasant soul. When it comes right down to it I don't think he has the courage to make a new kind of ruling.

"Some new cases are coming up before the Supreme Court which have some extension of civilian protection and constitutional rights but not in the military courts. They just won't rule in any new way. The military appellate level is such that if you receive a conviction at the trial level it means that you undergo your sentence because they don't stay your sentence pending appeal and the appeal takes a long time. By the time you get through you've already done your time.

"I got the distinct impression that Judge Nichols had a conscience but generally ruled against it. He knew what was right but ignored it for his own convenience. I was personally harassed by some MPs. You know they had never seen any lawyers who looked like I do. They bothered me and Nichols sent word from the bench to the General that if they did any more of that he was going to haul the General in himself.

"I would drive down every day and as I came into the court one morning, the old guards were getting too friendly with the defendants so they had a change to some white hats who were brought up from Fort Meade or something like that. I came in at about 8:00 A.M. and I wanted to see my client. I wanted to talk to him before the day's trial began and they wouldn't let me see him. They said, 'Are you a lawyer?' and I said: 'Yeah' and they said: 'Some identification?' and I said: 'Well I just don't carry my diploma with me. It's not a habit I have.' I said: 'I have lawyer tattooed on my chest but that wouldn't mean anything.' Essentially they just wouldn't let me see him and threatened physical interference at which point I just walked out in a steam. I didn't want to get into a fistfight with a couple of guards. I came into court and I was really livid. It was in the pre-trial hearing. I jumped up and down on the record and Nichols really got mad and bawled Anzaldi out. That was the kind of issue he could deal with."

Compared to Attorney Vladeck, Cohn felt he had no trouble about his treatment as defense counsel. He knew the people down there. His comment was: "They may have treated her [Vladeck] differently. It may have been male chauvinism. Every day after trial if I said I want a couple of hours with my client they would keep him there.

"I had no trouble with Anzaldi because I realized early in the game the way to handle Anzaldi was to get him mad at you at which point he had no control. He had no self-control. He dug his own grave. He was constantly being reprimanded by the judge. I made one motion to remove him because of prejudice since he had served as Klug's defense lawyer. I made the point in a particularly abrasive way. I called Hank as a witness and Anzaldi responded in such a way that it became evident that if I made personal jabs he would over-respond.

"He apologized to me at the end of the trial for being what he was, essentially a pig, and I told him that it was his choice to be a pig, not mine and I didn't want to deal with that. But he's now defense counsel out there again and he's very anxious to do a creditable job. Again you have to go through a detailed analysis of what makes a liberal prosecutor and I think he is a liberal prosecutor.

"Guys like Anzaldi are caught in a lot of conflicts in their own position, so they tend to flail out blindly.

"You'll find that most of the people in the JAG office these days see themselves as liberal, most of them are antiwar, at least most of the ones I've met. The defense lawyers are liberal and antiwar. The pro-war people gravitate to prosecutors on the whole. They have some choice. For instance the guy who functioned as my co-counsel in the Catlow case, a lovely guy, a very fine lawyer, told them, he said: 'You make me a prosecutor . . .' (you see what they tend to do in the military is take the guys who win the most cases and make them prosecutors), '. . . and I'm just going to lose cases. I'll throw it. I can't conceive of being a prosecutor, so don't do it. You'll lose a lot of cases that way so don't do it.' So they didn't. They sent him to Vietnam. Hank's co-counsel also went to Vietnam."

Tom Catlow was sentenced to a dishonorable discharge

on November 23, 1970. But Tom's struggle with the Army did not end with his sentencing. Normally after a dishonorable discharge, since this sentence involves no prison time, a prisoner would be granted extended leave awaiting the automatic appeal. With Tom Catlow the Army made new rules and refused to discharge him but transferred him to PCF [Personnel Control Facility],* illegally denied him all pay and subjected him to increased harassment. He was told by PCF guards that the Army was deliberately stalling his release.

Meanwhile Tom's 14-year-old stepbrother, of whom he had grown increasingly fond, was stricken with muscular dystrophy and on top of that came down with bronchitis. Tom's mother was desperate for funds. The state refused to come through with hospitalization and while the family was suing the state they were destitute. Through the months of beatings and brutalities in the stockade Tom had remained helpless while he watched others driven to suicide attempts. With the tragedy of his brother's illness, his mother's money worries and his own new sense of manhood Tom was determined to strike out. When he became aware of the Army's refusal to give him what any other prisoner under the same circumstances would get, excess leave, he simply extended his Christmas leave and went AWOL from December 29, 1969 up until his dishonorable discharge was reversed. He took every job he could find, worked as a filing clerk and mailing clerk in an office. He loaded and unloaded freight cars for the Key Food Company. He worked as freelance mover and carpenter, sometimes holding several of these jobs at once, contributing his earnings to pay for his brother's hospital bills.

On September 22, 1971, the Army Court of Military Appeals overturned Tom's conviction for riot and arson on the grounds that he had been held incommunicado for four days following the rebellion, that all rights to counsel had been denied him. The court went further to state that even if Catlow's right to counsel had been respected there was enough evidence of guard brutality during the CID interrogation as to make any statement or confession invalid.

The reversal of Tom's dishonorable discharge on the riot charges automatically turned Tom into a soldier again with time to do on his original AWOL charge for which he had been placed in the stockade before the riot. The seven months he had spent in Segregation awaiting his riot court-martial didn't count by the Army's perverse rules. Tom decided to turn

* See "Afterword: The Cage."

himself in voluntarily while awaiting another trial on his original AWOL. His attorneys were building their case on the incontestable evidence that Tom had been falsely inducted by both the military and civilian laws.

Tom granted a special television interview over NBC on September 30, 1971 on the subject of deserters. He held a press conference at the Washington Square Methodist Church explaining that he was turning himself into the Army on his original AWOL charges hoping to get out of the service for once and for all. The Fort Dix authorities immediately granted Tom an extended leave and told the press that Tom's request for an undesirable discharge on the AWOL charge (in lieu of being court-martialed) was being processed. For eight weeks the Army lived up to its word and treated Tom as they would have any other soldier under the same circumstances. Tom was allowed the freedom of the base and leave to go home.

On November 15th when he arrived at PCF (holding facility) he was summoned to the guard house and ordered to the stockade. He asked why he was being thrown in the stockade and was told that the authorities had decided that there was too much paper work involved in signing him in and out of PCF. At this point he could still leave the base without escort to make phone calls from Wrightstown. When he returned voluntarily from such a sortie he was thrown into Seg, with no explanation, and for the next week he was treated like public enemy number one, the only prisoner in his section of the cell block. All other prisoners in further reaches of the corridor had to be locked in their cells when he was let out to shave, shower or get his fifteen minutes of exercise. When Colonel Craighead, the new Commander of the stockade came by on his tour he told Tom that he had heard about him and that he had read his file and considered him a dangerous prisoner. Tom's attorneys and Clariss* were frantic. For twenty-four hours they had no idea where Tom was and the Army refused all information as to his whereabouts. When the Inspector General came through Tom complained to him about his unjust imprisonment but the Inspector General said he was sorry there was nothing he could do about it.

Just as mysteriously, two and a half weeks after Tom's total segregation Tom was let out of Seg and returned to the compound of the stockade.

On January 7th, Tom's trial came up for his two year AWOL. The trial started at nine in the morning and ended at eleven forty-five in the evening. Judge Nichols was no longer

* Clariss Ritter Catlow, Tom's wife; and see p. 100.

practicing at Dix. He had been sent to Vietnam and Lieutenant Colonel Robert W. Morrison presided as judge.

At the beginning of the proceedings the Judge and Tom's defense attorney had a verbal exchange worthy of Kafka, Gilbert and Sullivan and *Alice in Wonderland:*

JUDGE MORRISON: The court is aware of the practice in the civilian courts of encouraging people under charges, if they are of military age, to join the military service. And we know recruiters are available to fill their quotas in that way. And, the military judge is personally aware that this practice goes on and has even been a party to it in other years. And it is the practice, on my personal knowledge, in Illinois courts, where this has happened. Where I have been present the [civilian] charges are withdrawn when the accused has taken the oath or enlisted in the Army or the Navy, or some other military service. And this has become such a common practice over the years that I'm almost invited to say since there are no longer any known charges pending against the accused by the New Jersey Courts or New Jersey Juvenile Courts that this, in fact, was done. As you say, your record as you sought, showed dismissal five days later; when it was learned, I presume, that the accused was in the Army. Now, your point is that because charges were still pending and had not been stricken from the record that the Army could not waive its own procedures and induct or enlist this accused.

DEFENSE ATTORNEY CURTIS McCLANE: That's correct, sir.

MILITARY JUDGE: Therefore, the whole thing has been vitiated and he has never been a soldier.

D.A. McCLANE: That's right.

That a military judge should complacently admit for the record that not only is the practice of illegal induction common, but that he as a civilian judge practiced it in Illinois, is one more pathetic example of the sloughs of immorality to which our military and civil justices have sunk.

Unfortunately for Tom he was not "vitiated" as a soldier, but at midnight he was returned to the stockade and thrown into Seg. Then without any warning early the morning of January 12th he was picked up, handcuffed, processed out and flown with two guards on a civilian flight to Fort Leavenworth, Kansas. He had no chance to call his wife or attorney who spent another anxious twenty-four hours trying to locate him. Clariss wrote General Cooksey and General Hennessee, the officer in charge of Leavenworth, pleading with them for Tom's release, explaining that she was pregnant, had had a recent miscarriage, wanted to hold onto this baby and needed Tom badly. Tom wrote letters to General Hennessee and General Cooksey asking to apply his seven months pre-trial confinement in the stockade toward this current sentence and at the very least to give him twenty-three days clemency so he could be home with Clariss to help her with the birth of the baby. In a surprise move Fort Leavenworth sent a Red Cross worker to interview Tom's mother on the whole sad story. Tom's mother was vehement about never sending another son into the services, and how under no conditions would she ever again sign enlistment papers.

On March 31st Tom was told that he would be released on April 3rd. Tom got out on excess leave on April 18, 1972, and started working for the Federation of Jewish Philanthropies as caretaker for a day care center. His case will be tried on a writ of habeas corpus (on the grounds that his induction was illegal) before a Federal Court and the findings there will take precedence over all military courts.

Tom Catlow's illegal punishment by the military in 1972 after his voluntary return; his arbitrary imprisonments, his treatment as a dangerous criminal demonstrated how deeply the Fort Dix uprising affected the highest military authorities. Though the civilian world may have forgotten the riot, if more than a small percentage were ever aware of it, though the official army Post paper pretends it never happened, there is now no doubt that the military elite has not forgotten. They remain deeply shaken and vindictive.

BILL BRAKEFIELD

**There are some who cluck and wonder what the nation has
done to deserve Johnson and Humphrey and Wallace and
Nixon. My question is different. What have we done to deserve
Bill Brakefield and from where does he come? What mystery is
there in this society and in the human soul that we can find a
Bill Brakefield in our midst . . . ?**

— ***Win*** **magazine, October, 1968**

This panegyric was written by David McReynolds, not
about Bill Brakefield the pacifist awaiting a court-martial verdict
in the Fort Dix stockade, undergoing starvation and beatings
with a thirty-year prison sentence hanging over his head, but
about an earlier Bill Brakefield, the nineteen-year-old private
who took sanctuary at City College on October 31, 1968.

David McReynolds has been a pacifist all his life. He was
the founder of the New York Resistance; more recently he was
the delegate from the War Resisters League to the International
Federation for Disarmament and Peace in London. Dave met
Bill initially very late the first evening of Bill's sanctuary in the
C.C.N.Y. Finley Student Center ballroom. He gives a vibrant picture of the quiet, resolute young man who came to his own
singular moral position in the middle of inner and outer
confusion.

"The ballroom was a cheery, rather mindless shambles of
students playing Frisbee, wandering around, reading, listening
to rock records, eating, sitting, lying, talking. In the midst of this
was Bill Brakefield . . . in the midst of all this noise he was terribly alone. The Frisbee players would not be going to jail except
for a brief period when they resisted the impending arrest. He
faced a court-martial and military prison. He was nineteen . . .
he was taking sanctuary but he was unwilling for a single person to be hurt. I asked him what brought him to his position and
he began to discuss the war and how he felt it was wrong; and
I said no, that wasn't what I meant—I wanted to know why he
had moved beyond merely opposing the war to the concept of
dealing gently even with the police. He could not really answer;
it was something that had come from within him. And there at

nineteen he sat, frightened, serious, knowing what awaited him."

On the following evenings a host of professional people and established poets dropped by to pay their respects to Bill, among them Ed Sanders, Paul Blackburn, Allen Ginsberg, the late Alfred Conrad, Adrienne Rich. Some of the poets gave impromptu readings. In Bill's words:

"I met all these people for the first time at my sanctuary. I met the late Professor Alfred Conrad there. He offered his support and spoke a few times for me and about me. He and his wife, the poetess Adrienne Rich, became lasting friends of mine, as did Allen Ginsberg, with whom I'm still corresponding, and Dave McReynolds. It was *my* sanctuary. It wasn't people using me. I had the choice of how it was going to be when the police came to make their bust, how the people were going to act. I don't know the names of the people who were in the Students for a Democratic Society, except that there were some of them who wanted to barricade the building and I didn't agree with their philosophy. I got to know the ins and outs of police undercover agents. There were quite a few there at my sanctuary. There was one old black man who was made to look like a Skid Row drunk and he came to cause trouble, but the night of the bust he suddenly sobered up and was talking to the chief of police. There were two young officers who had several days' growth of beard who were placed in the paddy wagon with us when we were taken to the police station; these two had been loudest, trying to scare some of the first offenders by saying that we'd get beat up or that they'd take our clothes away from us, but they disappeared before anyone else.

"I spent seven days in the ballroom, from Halloween night to November 6th. There were approximately two hundred people when the bust came. There were pacifists; there were Students for a Democratic Society. I wanted it to be as pacific as possible. I had my way. The doors were kept open and the police when they came met no trouble at all."

On Sunday, November 3rd, Bill went out to address a rally. While he was gone a group of plainclothes detectives appeared at the City College sanctuary. They asked for Private William S. Brakefield. Though they had no warrant for his arrest, they said they had come to advise him of *his* rights and to advise him to return to his Army base, but since Bill was not there they left.

On Monday, November 4th, the plainclothes detectives reappeared at the ballroom, this time accompanied by policemen. They handcuffed Bill Brakefield while advising him of his rights and advising him to return to his Army base.

Clariss Ritter, a dedicated young administrative and legal assistant to the Workers Defense League, was then working for the New York Resistance. She had been counseling Bill as an AWOL soldier before the sanctuary; she participated in the sanctuary from the beginning. Clariss remembers that she and others gathered students from the street and the halls of C.C.-N.Y., jammed the ballroom, and then told the detectives that they couldn't spirit Bill away like that; it would have to be through or over all their live bodies. The chief detective kept running to the door and then back to the quiet seated figure of Bill Brakefield. Finally the detectives gave up. They unhandcuffed Bill and left.

On Wednesday, November 6th, one week after Bill had walked into the ballroom, 250 helmeted police from the New York police Tactical Patrol Force arrived at C.C.N.Y. and headed for the Finley Student Center. Dean James A. Peace addressed the students through a bull horn. He was surrounded by plainclothes police. He told the students that if they left immediately no charges would be brought against them. The young people sitting on the floor of the ballroom shouted: "Hell no, we won't go." A young man from the group advised that anyone who did not want to be arrested had better leave immediately. A few young people left. At 1:27 P.M. Bill Brakefield was carried out peacefully. The newspapers reported that military police had been seen on campus but that they had left the arresting to the city police.

Gerald Lefcourt and Michael Kennedy, from the Emergency Civil Liberties Committee, advised the students of their rights. Kennedy was Bill's lawyer; on his advice the group decided not to post bail for Bill or for David Kopp, an AWOL serviceman who had not declared himself in public sanctuary but who was absent without leave from the Air Force. At one point during Bill's sanctuary David had burned his Air Force identification card. Kennedy explained that if the group posted bail for the servicemen, military police would pick them up immediately, the bail money would be lost, and more important, if and when the two finally did get out of military custody they would have a criminal offense pending against them in New York City.

About 150 sympathizers were taken to precincts all over the city, arrested on criminal charges with misdemeanors pending, photographed and let go. The police took Bill and David to the

Tombs and then to Rikers Island. For Bill, "That was a new experience. It was the first time that I had been in a civilian jail. I got to know the Black Panthers for the first time. Everyone at Rikers Island had only the clothes that were on their backs when they'd been picked up. Those were the only clothes they had to wear. There were people there who had been in for six months still wearing the same clothes. There were sixteen-year-old kids mixed in with hardened criminals, the four- or five-time losers, and the kids would be there for stealing a hubcap or some such minor offense. It was a holding place where people stayed until their trials came up. One man and his two sons were being held for attempting to assassinate Nixon. They were on the other side of the cell block from me. The New York City police had busted into their house, found a high-powered rifle, and decided they were assassins. The men were Arabs, I believe."

On November 13th, Bill was brought before Judge Thomas G. Weaver in Manhattan. Judge Weaver found him guilty of criminal trespass in the third degree, but in delivering the verdict the judge stated: "I admire your motives and your objectives. I hope all demonstrations in the future are as peaceful as yours." He sentenced Bill to the seven days which Bill had already spent at Rikers Island. Bill was then taken into military custody.

"I was taken to Fort Dix by bus along with all the other AWOL soldiers who had been picked up that morning. At Fort Dix I was placed in Area B. A Area is inside the fence of the stockade, but it's minimum custody. Prisoners in A Area are allowed to work on the outside under unarmed guards. Area B is the second lowest grade. Segregation is the lowest. I was the first of [what was to become] the Fort Dix Thirty-Eight to arrive in the stockade. I knew nothing of Terry [Klug] or of Jeff [Russell] or of the American Servicemen's Union, but that first night I met two other prisoners, whose names I've forgotten. We agreed politically that we weren't going to serve the Army, that there was certainly no use in cooperating in the stockade. The next night we were put in Segregation on Disciplinary Segregation diet: The regulation states that they can keep you on D.S. chow for fourteen days, then back to normal food for fourteen days and then back again to D.S. chow for fourteen, for a total of eighty days on the diet. If you do that time they can no longer put you on D.S. chow. I was on D.S. chow the full limit. A doctor is supposed to give you a physical before you are placed on this diet; the doctor would come by but he would stand outside our cells and check off all the statistics without examining us.

"November 15, 1968, I started my long year in Segregation. In January Terry Klug came over from France and right into Fort Dix Seg. I learned that he was very involved in American Servicemen's Union work; unionizing soldiers for better wages, better treatment, no more yes-sirring and no-sirring of officers, better treatment for the Black and Puerto Rican soldiers. John Lewis, another ASU member, was in the stockade at that time, and there were about five or six Swedish deserters—soldiers who had deserted to Sweden but returned to America. After meeting Terry and learning about the ASU, I joined. We talked to the officers. We tried to ask them why there was a caste system; why did officers expect to be treated better; why, if they didn't get the respect that they felt they were owed, did they feel people had to be punished so severely.

"I lost forty pounds in Seg. The longest stretch I spent was six months, with twelve days in and out of the compound. As soon as they saw me talking to fellow prisoners back I'd go into Seg. I kept my pacifist beliefs. I refused to serve and refused to fight back when I got roughed up. There I differ from the ASU members."

On July 4, 1969, Bill wrote a letter to the ASU paper, *The Bond,* asking the readers to write their Congressmen and Senators about the conditions at Dix:

> Abraham Lincoln once said, "To sin by silence when they know they should protest makes cowards of men." I am not a coward; neither are the four other young men who along with myself are being brought before a general court-martial on conspiracy charges for the riot here at Ford Dix stockade June 5, 1969.

> I wish to protest the inhuman treatment we have and are enduring since June 5th. It was the inhuman treatment which caused the rebellion of sixty black, Puerto Rican, and white prisoners here at the stockade!

> On June 6, 1969, I was brought down to Segregation; some of my friends were already here; some had not yet been brought to Segregation. Here is a rough idea of the sort of treatment I received. With three guards in front of me, three behind, and two on either side of me holding on to my arms, I was shoved violently through

the door of Segregation Cell Block 77. I was pushed against the wall, spread-eagle fashion. I was then searched for any weapon I may have concealed (what had I done?) on my person. My arms and legs started to shake involuntarily, my face contorted with the time and strain as the minutes dropped like sweat from my brow. All the while the guards told me not to move or they would enjoy beating my face into the cold concrete floor of the cell block.

Finally, after what seemed like hours, a sergeant grabbed my collar at the back of my neck and pulled me up to a standing position. My knees buckled but I could not go to the floor for these pigs; I stayed erect. I was told to get into the shower room and strip. After I had stripped naked and my anus and penis had been checked for possible razor blades to be used against an "innocent guard" I was told to stand in the shower stall. Another sergeant came over to talk to me. He said: "Brakefield, a policeman is going to shoot you dead one of these days." I was going to tell him violence is the tool of the ignorant but I kept my mouth shut.

For the first forty-eight hours all the prisoners who were pending investigation were kept on Disciplinary Segregation. This is punishment; we had done nothing to deserve this. We were not allowed to smoke, to write, or to speak to anyone . . .

Having come from the South, Bill was very sensitive to racism. One of the specific barbarities that made him bitter was the guards' treatment of blacks in the stockade:
"The guards were particularly sadistic with the blacks in the stockade. They would call them 'black monkey' or 'nigger.' They'd taunt them with: 'You mad at me, nigger?' 'You want to come jump on me?' Sometimes the guards would just go into black prisoners' cells and beat them up. Soldiers who were supposed to be mature enough to rank E7 would go into a prisoner's cell at night and beat him up while he slept. This went on all the time. One incident happened to Terry and me while we were on D.S. chow. In Segregation one prisoner is let out to serve the other prisoners. The prisoner brings the tray to your door. This time the prisoner told us that he had been forced to serve Terry and me with water from the toilet; the

guards had said that if he didn't he would be roughed up. Water was very important to us then; it was the only liquid we got. There was no action we could take. We just didn't drink the water.

"I became known in the stockade because of my long term in Segregation. Other prisoners began to realize that I was trying to change things. They got to know my face from the times I was taken to chapel. They began to know what I stood for.

"I used to submit six or seven 5-10s a day—5-10s were request slips to complain about just such incidents as the toilet water, but it was like *Catch 22:* most of the time the guards would take the slips and throw them away before they ever got to Major Casey or Major Cashman. If a slip did get to Major Casey, he would read the request in front of my cell, tell me there was nothing he could do about it, and throw it away. After the riot, when they took all privileges away from us, I wrote out 5-10s asking that we be allowed to receive books from publishers, be allowed to attend church, be allowed to receive newspapers, be allowed to attend weekend movies. Nothing happened until our lawyers, Hank DiSuvero and Rowland Watts, received the manual for the guidance of prisoners from Washington; then the officers at Fort Dix discovered that we were supposed to be allowed such privileges.

"Then there were the straps. I was never put in the straps myself, but I was witness to their use on other prisoners. Going out for my fifteen minutes of exercise I saw guards putting men in straps, or coming back from my fifteen minutes of exercise I'd pass a cell where a prisoner was arched in his straps. When we got word out to the outside world, the straps would be hidden for a while and stockade officials would deny using them; then back they'd go to putting men in straps again. Major Casey must have known about the straps. He had to give the order to use them."

After the riot, while in Seg, Bill wrote this piece for *The Bond:*

> Having been confined for eight months in the Fort Dix stockade as a political prisoner because of my beliefs, activities, and convictions, it has been my pleasure to have met some pretty interesting and fairly disgusting men of rank.
>
> Please take for example one person, a Sergeant E6.

This Sergeant has asked me repeatedly to get his name in print. Eyery day, as the Sergeant tours Seg, he jokes with me about writing him up in an underground, anti-military/establishment newspaper that is located outside the Fort Dix area.

Today the Sergeant came through the cell blocks and passed up my cell completely. One of the guards who was passing through with the Sergeant turned to me and said the Sergeant wasn't speaking to me because I had hurt his feelings.

This man, Sergeant E6 Howard (Howie) Davidson, whose feelings are so easily hurt because his name does not appear in print, has many times disregarded the feelings of others.

Howie has a particularly disgusting habit of putting people in straps. He thoroughly enjoys this practice of medieval torture.

Straps consist of putting a prisoner on his stomach, putting your knee (in Howie's case this is over two hundred pounds of pressure) in the small of the prisoner's back to hold him down, then taking his arms and legs and strapping them together somewhere up behind the shoulder blades. Howie then "likes" to laugh and say, "talk back to me now motherfucker! ha, ha."

Well, Howie, I have finally written you up. I hope the people who read this can picture the type of military policeman you and the majority of your friends are.

—William Steven Brakefield

Bill was born in San Diego, California, March 2, 1949. His father, Lester Brakefield, was a Chief Petty Officer E7 in the Navy. Bill's paternal grandfather was beaten up in 1920 by a Klansman because he helped black people in the rural section of Alabama.

Bill's mother was originally from California, although born in Canada. Her mother is a Scotch Livingston, a great granddaughter of the famous Dr. Livingston. Bill's maternal grandfather was American, Welsh by descent. He fought in World

War I, was wounded, couldn't enlist in the U.S. Army in World War II, so he enlisted in Canada.

Bill's father, Lester, was a heavy drinker, drunk for one week out of every month. Six months after Bill's birth, Lester left the Navy and moved the whole family to Jasper, Alabama. Lester and his brother built a shack in which Bill, his three older brothers, older sister, mother, and father lived. It had a tin roof, pot-bellied stove and an outhouse. When Bill was of school age he wore his brothers' hand-me-down clothes and walked barefoot to school, a one-room school with pot-bellied stove and outhouse.

Alabama schools and buses were completely segregated while Bill was growing up. The Brakefields had no religion but Mrs. Brakefield had strong ethical convictions. Bill remembers going to town with his mother and sitting in the back of the bus with the blacks.

Lester had been working in the Bethlehem steel mill in Birmingham, Alabama but his brother seemed to be doing better at the steel plant in Buffalo, so in 1957 the Brakefields moved to Cheektoga, New York, three miles from Buffalo. Lester was still drinking heavily. He received a pension from the Navy once a month, and as Bill remembers it, like clockwork—his father would go on a binge the first week of every month. Bill's memories of this period are bitter:

"If my father hadn't kicked my mother on a drunk when she was pregnant, I would have had a baby brother or sister. On another drunk he broke her fingers. It got so bad that my mother would disappear, go downtown when my father was drunk, leaving us to fend for ourselves at home. We would lock ourselves in our rooms, barricade the door, and live on crackers and juice until my father got over his drunk. He was arrested one time for urinating out of doors, and spent six months in jail.

"When I was fourteen I found out that I could read better and faster than the others in my class. I was reading on a twelfth-grade level. I was bored with the way I was being taught. I dropped out of school. I weighed 198 pounds—I ate a lot because I was worried about my home. I was six feet tall. I was the biggest member of the family. One night my father came downstairs from sleeping off a binge, still somewhat drunk. It was about 9:00 on a Sunday evening. He was smoking a cigarette. He put the cigarette out on my kneecap. I snapped. All the years before we had always run when he was drunk. This was the first time any child of his fought back. I got up and pulled my father up. I hit him once, and then I started crying, which I had never done before. (I could never cry as a kid.)

"I went into a state of semishock. I refused to talk and I couldn't blink my eyes. I was taken to a hospital, where I talked with a psychiatrist and immediately snapped out of it. I poured out sixteen years of feeling.

"After that I lived with my sister, who was home from the Air Force with her child. I stayed in downtown Buffalo with her until the next school year. I was dissatisfied and disinterested, and decided to go back down South where I knew the school systems were behind, so that if I reentered the eleventh grade I could complete it. I went back to Jasper and lived with my father's sister. Her husband, who had helped build our house when we first moved to Jasper, had died. So I was living with her, helping her, helping her to overcome her shock plus going to school, hoping to complete the eleventh grade and then go back to Buffalo so I could graduate with my peer group.

"During the eight years I lived in New York my ideas about integration and segregation, my political ideas, had grown so that I didn't like it in Alabama anymore. No one taught me about philosophy, religion or the Bible. I started reading on my own. Back in 1965 or 1966 I wasn't involved with gangs, with high-heeled boots and black leather jackets. I could see that those people were 'following,' and I could never be like that. I usually kept to myself. The part in my hair I've had since I combed my own hair. The way I dress is my own.

"Back South I dropped out of high school for the second time. My parents moved back to Birmingham, where my father went back to work in the steel mills. He'd been fired from his job in New York for drunkenness. In Birmingham I attended Phillips High School, where there were Black students. There was prejudice, a different kind of prejudice from the rural South. Colored folk lived in their shanties, poor whites lived in theirs, and they attended different schools. People couldn't relate to each other's poorness.

"After I dropped out of school for the third time in Birmingham, I learned about the Job Corps at a meeting, and I enrolled. One of the requirements for entering the Job Corps is that your family must make $2,000 a year or less. My family made less, so I was eligible. I stayed in the Job Corps for a year and a month.

"The Job Corps was set up to teach skills to people who were from sixteen years of age to twenty-one, and to help them with their education. I studied as a clerk typist; I became an assistant teacher for the high school equivalency exam; and a recruiter. I went to Detroit, Chicago and cities in between speaking to groups about the Job Corps. In the Job Corps I began to develop skills that I hadn't known I had. I was selected by the other foremen—of whom the majority were black and Eskimo—to be the leader. I was a barracks leader. It was the best time of my life. I was liked by blacks and Puerto Ricans and other white people.

"Although I was a high-school dropout, I was used as an example. Articles were submitted about me to the OEO office in Washington. I passed an entrance examination to Western Michigan University.

"While in the Job Corps I had worked at a hospital for mentally retarded children, and enjoyed the work. At WMU I hoped to become a special education teacher. I've always been interested in teaching. But at WMU I became disinterested. English was my best subject, but I was bored by the way it was being taught. I dropped out to enlist in the Army. The Army tests showed that I could go through OCS, but I chose the Army Security Agency. I didn't want to be a foot soldier. I had growing feelings about the horror of killing.

"I used to buy pencils from blind men and talk to drunks or anybody in trouble. I never knew how much I cared until after I got in the Army; then it was too late. But I grew rapidly and became politically aware.

"At Fort Devons I found a friend who felt the same way I did about killing, Rudy Poe. We read Hesse together and discussed our beliefs openly; as a result we were given extra details. Rudy refused to wear his uniform and I went AWOL for twenty-three days in March, 1968. I landed in the Fort Devons stockade, but because that was overcrowded I was sent to the Fort Dix stockade. There I was placed in A Compound, but I refused to cooperate and was placed in Segregation. I suffered severe anxiety my first time in the Fort Dix solitary cell. I was sent to Fort Monmouth, because the Dix stockade was overcrowded. At Fort Monmouth I quickly became a parolee and was sent to Fort Hancock, where there were no bars and you could eat in a mess hall and work outdoors. In early September I was sent back to Fort Devons. I went AWOL again October 3rd, fed up with the mistreatment I had suffered for having strong pacifist convictions. I applied for a medical transfer.

"In October, 1968, I found out that they were not giving me the medical transfer, I was to become a foot soldier, I went

AWOL to New York. I picked New York because I had read about organizations there that helped soldiers. New York Resistance appealed to me. I picked up a *Village Voice,* saw the number to call, and did. Three weeks later I took sanctuary at City College."

From a stockade population of over seven hundred, of which 250 prisoners rioted, Bill Brakefield, the pacifist, was one of the five singled out by the Army's Criminal Investigation Division for court-martial. He was accused of fomenting the riot, of setting a fire and of throwing a footlocker out the window. His court-martial was tried on the 9th, 10th, 11th, 12th, 15th and 16th of December, 1969.

Despite the fact that the witnesses against Brakefield were extremely shaky, either not standing up to their sworn CID statements or in very questionable psychological condition; despite the fact that on direct cross-examination every one of these prosecutor's witnesses answered that they had not seen Bill Brakefield commit any of the actions of which he was accused; despite the fact that Major Casey, who had signed a sworn statement that he had seen two Caucasians running the length of the building in which Brakefield was supposed to have set a fire, reconsidered on cross-examination and was not sure that he could tell whether they were Caucasians or blacks; despite the fact that Brakefield had very strong character witnesses to the seriousness and depth of his nonviolent beliefs, Bill Brakefield was sent to Leavenworth for three years with a bad conduct discharge, forfeiture of all pay and allowances.

This verdict struck Dr. Arthur Weinberg of Woodmere, New York and Sergeant Robert J. Smith of the United States Air Force as so monstrously unfair that they independently pleaded with the highest authorities. Both these men were decorated soldiers.

Dr. Weinberg, previously Chief Consultant to the United States Air Force hospital at Mitchell Field, had a letter of high commendation. He included this letter with the letter he addressed to the Commanding General of Fort Dix, General Collins on December 18, 1969:

> In the name of our only child, Ann, who died at the age of twenty-one in a fatal automobile accident . . . I have followed the court-martial of Private William Brakefield with grave concern and am deeply distressed by the

sentence of three years which was imposed by the court . . .

My knowledge of the character of Bill Brakefield comes from my daughter, who knew Bill well before he entered the Fort Dix stockade. I am writing this letter in her behalf because just two days before she met with her fatal automobile accident on August 25, we discussed with her the events that took place in the Fort Dix stockade in June, sixteen days before Bill was to be released. Her evaluation of Bill, resulting from her friendship and experience with him before and during the sanctuary at City College, was that it was not in his nature to participate in any act of violence. At the sanctuary he made every effort to protect his five hundred supporters and the arresting officers from bodily injuries, imploring that everybody leave peacefully and not to confront the arresting officers. . . .

We understand that any person under physical or emotional stress may deviate from his normal behavior; however, noting Bill's previous record and dedication to the principles of non-violence, it is impossible for my wife and I to believe that Private Brakefield would expose any human being to the danger of bodily injury. . . .

Dr. Weinberg went on to plead for a reduction of sentence in the name of his daughter and in keeping with the Christmas spirit. He sent a copy of this letter to the Secretary of the Army. He received no reply to either of his letters.

Sergeant Robert J. Smith of the 1607 United States Air Force Hospital was so enraged by the injustice of the sentence that he wrote a long personal letter to the President of the United States. He explained that up to this trial he had not believed what radical young people were saying about military justice:

During the month of December, 1969, I was transferred from my normal duty station at Dover AFB to McGuire Air Force Base in New Jersey, which is adjacent to Fort Dix. During this time I became acquainted with a number of young political radicals who had opened up a coffeehouse in the nearby community of Wrightstown. They described numerous alleged incidents of misuse of military authority by the officers and enlisted MPs at the Fort Dix stockade both prior to and following the June 5 riot. The local radicals also seemed convinced that the four "ring-leaders" were being tried and convicted on political grounds rather than on the basis of incriminating evidence. After a rather fruitless exchange of political viewpoints, I was challenged to attend the remaining two court-martials (Private Russell and Catlow had already been convicted) and decide for myself the nature of the evidence being presented and the fairness of the decisions being rendered. Since I had the free time available and it seemed unfair to dismiss their allegations without an objective appraisal, I agreed to attend. The trial of Terry Klug was uneventful. The government's case was not strong enough to warrant a conviction and after a short deliberation the jury voted for acquittal. The results justified my expectations. . . .

The trial of Private William Brakefield began the following week. It became rapidly apparent that the government's case was once again based primarily on guilt by association. Private Brakefield had spoken out strongly against the war in Vietnam, against what he considered widespread racism in the Army, and against poor conditions and ill-treatment of prisoners in the stockade. From the testimony given it seemed probable that Private Brakefield was in sympathy with the aims of the rioters and the prosecution seemed to feel that therefore he must have participated in the riot. There was, however, no creditable evidence presented to that effect. The only witness who directly linked Private Brakefield to the incident was a Mr. Arnett, who had been discharged from the service on psychiatric grounds a few months after the disturbance in question. Mr. Arnett stated that he saw someone that looked like Private Brakefield in the area of a recently started fire. Under defense cross-examination he was unable to make even a reasonably positive identification. Later in the trial, a defense witness, Dr. (Major) Litvak, who had psychiatrically interviewed Mr. Arnett on numerous occasions prior to his discharge, testified that the prosecution's witness was a "psychopathic liar"; and that Mr. Arnett might very well lie under oath in order to enhance his feelings of self-importance by being associated with a significant event such as a court-martial.

Dr. Litvak stated that he would not give Mr. Arnett's testimony credence under any circumstances.

After the jury retired I sat out in the waiting room and discussed the case and the forthcoming certain (in my mind) verdict with Private Brakefield's fiancee . . . She was depressed and extremely pessimistic about the pending outcome. I laughingly assured her that his acquittal was virtually certain and that our "Fascist-pig military machine" wasn't the nine-headed serpent she seemed to think it was. Thirty minutes later Private William Brakefield was convicted of riot and simple arson and sentenced to serve three years at hard labor in the federal penitentiary at Leavenworth, Kansas.

Since that time I have spoken at length with Private Brakefield's family, fiancee and friends. They bring up two points of significance, especially when viewed in the light of the questionable verdict. By all accounts, William Brakefield was an ardent, sincere pacifist who incorporated this philosophy into his daily life as well as into his political convictions. That he could set fire to an occupied building was universally inconceivable to his family and friends. . . .

A second germane fact not brought up at the trial was that at the time of the June 5 riot, Private Brakefield had but ten days left to serve on his AWOL conviction. . . . It seems unlikely that he would instigate or participate in a riot under these circumstances. . . .

Even more than the waning Vietnam conflict, incidents of this type, even if they occur as infrequently as I would hope, are the focal point for the growing radicalization and alienation of America's intellectual youth. Certainly in a country the size of the United States, judicial injustices will occur, regardless of the political/economic system under which we are governed. However a growing number of young people are becoming convinced that there is no *rapid* means of rectifying these inevitable errors under our established political system and that the only way legitimate grievances of this nature can be corrected is through a complete and possibly violent overhaul of our entire governmental

112

structure. The rallying cry is "When tyranny is law, revolution is the order!" It is highly desirable that this destructive trend be countered now while these radical groups are fragmented and relatively insignificant. . . .

I would like to make a personal appeal for Presidential intervention in the case of Private William Brakefield. This man has been erroneously imprisoned since his original release date of June 15, 1969. Much of this time has been spent in solitary confinement under extremely difficult conditions. Private Brakefield is a bonafide political prisoner who has never advocated violence in any form. That this condition should exist in our democratic society is intolerable, and all possible means should be used to effect its immediate correction.

Like Dr. Weinberg, Sergeant Smith received no answer to his pleas.

On October 31, 1970, Rowland Watts, Bill's civilian attorney, and Captain Ira J. Dembrow, appellate defense counsel from the Army, submitted an appeal to the Military Court of Review. In their summation they gave a poignant picture of the struggles of one American youth of conscience:

The accused at the time of the acts charged was twenty years of age. He enlisted in the Army after a successful career in the Job Corps that led to a scholarship at Western Michigan University. He had been forced through poverty and the extreme alcoholism of his father to drop out of high school in a small town in Alabama but had completed his high school requirements while in the Job Corps.

Up until the time he became a Conscientious Objector to participation in war his military record was excellent. Thereafter he received two court-martials for being Absent Without Leave. In neither of these absences did he attempt to flee the jurisdiction of the military. In the first he voluntarily returned to pursue an application for conscientious objector discharge. During the second he sought "symbolic sanctuary" in the City College of New York. There he received widespread support from students and some faculty members but forbade any violent acts to prevent his arrest for trespass by the New York City police, and specifically refused to flee from his responsibilities. While serving his sentence of confinement for the latter AWOL conviction he was permitted to leave the stockade without escort and travel to Alabama alone to attend his father's funeral. He voluntarily returned within the time allotted to him. At the time of the disturbance of 5 June, 1969, he was within sixteen days of completion of his sentence on 21 June, 1969.

At the clemency hearing following his conviction he testified in his own behalf as to his sincere and absolute belief in non-violence. Also testifying in his behalf was his mother; his sister, a former member of the United States Air Force; his brother, Chief Lester D. Brakefield, a career noncommissioned in the United States Navy; another brother, Airman Larry T. Brakefield, a member of the United States Air Force; the stockade Chaplain, Captain Ronald L. Malloy; and Professor Alfred Conrad of the City College of New York. All testified to the accused's deep sense of responsibility, absolute integrity, commitment to non-violence, and dedication to helping those who were even more underprivileged in childhood than he had been.

His admitted objection to the war in Vietnam and his outspoken complaints about conditions in the Fort Dix Stockade are believed to have improperly influenced the court in assessing the harsh sentence imposed.

Wherefore, taking into consideration that the accused has been confined in excess of sixteen months at this time, it is respectfully moved that further confinement and forfeiture be set aside. It is further respectfully moved that the accused's Bad Conduct Discharge be set aside also.

The lawyers' plea for clemency was turned down; Bill was sent to Leavenworth. He wrote the following two letters just before he left for Leavenworth.
    On December 26th he wrote his lawyers and friends:

> Excuse me for not writing sooner. I didn't because I just didn't feel like it.
> The following is the only way I can describe my feelings right now.

In the beginning, before my court-martial, I felt like I was battling the injustices that I could no longer stand.

Now, after being sentenced to three years and knowing that I have to be "good" for those three years, I, of course, feel slightly beat. But it is only a slight feeling.

Today Carlos was struck by a guard, Spec. 4 Goodman, and placed on code eleven (very dangerous person) behind the mesh. (Carlos hit back.)

Goodman and the other guards on the shift have taken a cat, tied it up by its hind feet and beat it unconscious, and then placed their heels on the cat's head causing . . . death. I don't want this to go on after I leave . . . or I'll be returning to the Dix stockade.

No, I am not beat. I will though behave while at Leavenworth.

Please get word to Terry about Carlos and please come down to see Carlos and I.

Thanks to all of you for what you have done for me.

Hank, Carlos' last words, as they took him over to the mesh cells, were, "Fuck a 200 discharge," so I think you should come down to see him.

Happy New Year,
Bill

On January 8, 1970 he wrote:

Dear Rowland and everyone:

Last night a guard got angry at me and put his left hand around my throat with his thumb of his left hand underneath my Adam's apple. The guard was in my cell and I was up against the wall.

I am non-violent, Rowland, and because of this I am not very well liked. But, as should be expected, I do get angry like quite a few other people. Although I got angry I did not strike back. The guard left my cell. ANYWAY NONVIOLENCE IS WHAT'S HAPPENING.

I may go to Leavenworth tomorrow. If I don't I will write you again from there.

Oh yes, there were photographers here today taking pictures of cells. I overheard one of them mention something about using the pictures in Trenton for a suit filed against five members of the government.

Peace to all,
Bill

115

CARLOS RODRIGUEZ TORRES

In a way going to a court-martial is very much like going to practice in a small Southern town. The entire power structure is white, very straight . . . Rodriguez got the worst sentence for doing the least . . . and his sentence is nothing more than a reflection of racism. There's no other explanation for it . . .

—Henry DiSuvero

Carlos Rodriguez Torres is tall, very thin, with a pleading look in his large dark eyes.

Carlos was the last of the "Fort Dix thirty-eight" to be tried. Originally he was to get a special court-martial. The major difference between a special court-martial and a general court-martial is that in a special court-martial the maximum sentence a defendant can be given is a six month stretch with a possible bad conduct discharge no matter how many separate charges are being filed, whereas in a general court-marital, each of the charges can bring a maximum of ten years consecutively, which is why each of the five young men charged with a general court-martial faced a possible thirty, forty, or fifty year sentence.

One of the many ironies in Carlos' case is that because of a *subsequent* assault on a prison guard, his Special was changed to a general court-martial. Henry DiSuvero, who had won an acquittal for Terry Klug, was Carlos' civilian counsel in his court-martial. DiSuvero claims that what the Army was saying to Carlos was in effect: " 'We think you're a bad man and because of something which happened later, we'll punish you for something that happened earlier.' The analogy [in a civil court] would be if a prosecutor decided to prosecute somebody for a misdemeanor and then the plaintiff committed a second misdemeanor, the prosecutor would then charge the plaintiff with a felony on the first one. Impossible in a civil court." DiSuvero maintains that the second prosecution in Carlos' case should never have occurred "because the normal way in which attacks of a minor nature, which is all he was charged with, are taken care of is by putting the person under Disciplinary Segregation. The only two prosecutions involving attacks on guards in recent history before Carlos' were evoked by the same guard, this was Hindman. Although he was a

Sergeant, he had no training as a correctional officer. He performed his role in a way which was designed to elicit prisoner reaction."

The most ironic factor in Carlos' case, and it was a case of endless ironies, was that he was released from Segregation just a little over an hour before the riot took place on June 5th, so he could hardly have been considered one of the ringleaders of the riot, nor was the testimony against him, even if believed, as incriminating as it had been for the other defendants—yet he got the worst sentence.

Rodriguez' court-martial hung on the evidence of one witness who claimed to have seen him throwing a mattress on a fire that the same witness claimed to have seen Catlow start. Catlow was convicted of riot; Rodriguez was not. Catlow got no time and Rodriguez got a sentence of four years.

Another irony, and a crucial one in Rodriguez' trial, is that there were two Rodriguezes. Already there had been a confusion on the part of the officers as to who was who. Carlos remembers his astonishment at the first confusion: "It was before the riot . . . They made a mistake and they released me on September 28, 1968, for no reason that I could figure. Captain McClendon, a black officer came up to me and told me, 'I hear you are getting out.' That stumped me. Nobody had said a word to me about it. I'm in my solitary cell. It's Saturday. I say, 'Oh, yeah? I'm supposed to be getting out? Okay.' and he left. Nobody else came. Nobody called me that day and I figured that what he was trying to do was to pick me up so that I would come down harder. The next Sunday I had a visitor. I went to see my visitor and the guard started giving me a hassle. I'd been there so long I knew what the rules were about visiting, but the guard pretended I didn't. So I told him, 'I know this already, man. You don't have to tell me.' While we're hassling, McClendon came in. He had these papers in his hand. He said, 'Shut your mouth. It wouldn't bother me to take ten days off your good conduct time.' I shut up. They released me [from the stockade]. That was the strangest thing. They just said I was released, no explanation. He gave me everything back, all the things they take from you when you enter Seg. That was on a Sunday. I went to New York on Monday night. When I came back Tuesday, everybody started telling me that they were going to reconfine me. They had gotten mixed up with the Rodriguezes. So I cut out before they could put me back in Seg. I stayed out for thirty some-odd days and then decided to come back and get it over with."

This might never have happened if the Army had let Carlos use his full name. Carlos felt very bitterly about the abreviation of his name: "Every American kid has only one last name, right? Smith, Jones, whatever it is, but people of Latin descent always carry their mother's and their father's name. When you join the Army, they want to Americanize you, so they drop off your last name, like it's not even there. My mother was Delias Torres. My father William Rodriguez Colonne and in Latin countries the mother's name comes last so I am Carlos Rodriguez Torres, but they wouldn't have it. There was this Sergeant Craig and when he'd give roll call he'd say: 'Give me your whole name.' So I'd give him my whole name and then he'd say: 'You understand what I mean when I say give me your whole name.' So one day when I came out with my whole name he said: 'Motherfucker, you understand me when I say give me your whole name,' and I said: 'Look here, you understand me, sir, you don't call me "motherfucker" unless you have the evidence.' Wow, he blew up." That incident ended with Carlos doing fourteen days in Disciplinary Segregation on "rabbit chow."

The mixup over the two Rodriguezes had further sad consequences for Carlos as no one really knew which Rodriguez stepped forward when Chambers, the prosecutor's only witness, made his identification. It was Chambers who claimed that he had seen Rodriguez throwing a mattress on a fire. Henry Di-Suvero felt very angry about Judge Nichols' handling of this case: "The fact was that at that point [Carlos' trial], I think, Judge Nichols was interested not in seeing that justice was done but in seeing that the government won its case. . . .

"I think that there were two main errors committed by the judge. One was that he decided that the line-up that took place as people were called back into the barracks [the night of June 5th after the riot] was not a line-up. The Supreme Court says that a person in a line-up has a right to have a lawyer present. The purpose of having a lawyer present is to make sure that the line-up is a fair one, and to ensure that if any identification takes place, it does in fact take place.

"No one knew which Rodriguez really stepped forward when Chambers made that identification. Chambers himself destroyed the first copy of his notes that he said he wrote when he made the identification. No one was there to observe the lighting conditions to check on that. There is disputed testimony as to who called the roll. There's disputed testimony from government witnesses as to how many people were in the area in which the roll was called. All of these are problems that a fair line-up would alleviate by the presence of a lawyer. The refusal of the judge to hold that it was a line-up just because the person had always been in the custody of the police is, I think, very wrong. And if that identification had been discounted, the government would have had no case at all.

"The other error on the Judge's part in my opinion, was that we moved to permit the court to take a view of the barracks at sunset, because the key to the prosecution case was the ability of Chambers to make that identification at sunset. The government opposed it on the grounds that the light at sunset was different in January than in June. It may be different, but once the sun sets, the sun sets and it doesn't seem to me that there's that much difference. The other reason that they gave was that the lighting conditions in the stockade proper may have changed since then, but they presented no proof that, in fact, the lighting conditions had been changed. If we had been able to bring that court [jury] to those premises and shown them that no positive identification could be made eighty feet back into the barracks where the lights are off as the sun is setting and all you can see are shadows, the government's case would have been shot. The Judge took the government's position. Usually the shoe is on the other foot as in the Klug trial where the prosecution is trying to get in evidence and the defense is trying to keep out evidence. What we were trying to do in Rodriguez' case was to get in evidence. The government wasn't interested in the pursuit of truth. They were interested in a conviction, and that's what they got.

"I think that the real reason why Rodriguez was prosecuted as a general court-martial is that soon after the riot his picture was taken along with three others in a clenched fist salute. It was after this picture appeared in *The Bond* that he was prosecuted and charged for the subsequent assault and the initial recommendation that his case be a special court-martial was changed to a general court-martial."

Another interesting element in the Rodriguez court-martial was in the choosing of the court [the jury]. DiSuvero felt that right there, in the beginning, there was evidence of a special bias.

"One thing was that we had younger people in the Klug court and we had a black guy in the Klug court. Also, interestingly enough, I think in the Rodriguez trial it was the first time it was done in this series of cases, that the government exercised a preemptory challenge against one of the court

119

members. Usually the government does not exercise any preemptory challenge but the defense does. One reason for this is that the government never feels compelled to exercise a preemptory challenge in a military court because they're so sure of the caliber of people that they have on the court. It's not like in a jury case where the government will exercise its preemptories in very much the same way that the defense will, because the government realizes that certain people are hostile to their position. But generally the government knows that that's not the case in a military court. In the Rodriguez case, where the court is composed of officers not enlisted men, they weren't even going to take that chance. The one person who appeared to be very sympathetic [to Carlos] from the voir dire was the person who had the preemptory exercised against him."

Carlos grew up on the Lower East Side of New York City, Avenue D and Fourth Street, with his older sister and brother and his mother. When he was six and a half, his mother married his step-father. Shortly thereafter Carlos was sent away to boarding school to Saint Patrick's Military Academy. He ran away after a term and a half. He couldn't stand being locked up. By the time he was twelve he was snorting heroin. The way he remembers it: "Everybody was getting high there, smoking reefers, smoking dope, the works. You are what your environment is. I look back at my environment, the Lower East Side: drugs. Avenue D could stand for drugs. Yet my own brother and sister never messed with drugs and in a sense I blame it on myself.

"My mother didn't know what to do with me so first she sent me to live with an aunt in Queens but I'd keep sneaking back down to the Lower East Side of Manhattan.

"My real father lives in Puerto Rico. He has a clothing store there. I was twelve when my mother sent me to live with him. I went to school there. Everything was taught in Spanish. I didn't know Spanish that well. I was going to Puerto Rico and coming back to New York every six months. I'd start adjusting to the class in Puerto Rico, when it would be time to come back to New York and the same thing would happen here.

"My father never found me using drugs and I think he wanted me to stay in Puerto Rico and help him run the store. That was before my mother died. I was about thirteen and a half when my mother died. They brought me back from Puerto Rico. My mother was very sick in Saint Luke's Hospital. The last time I saw her was on December 22, 1963. She was unconscious. She died two days later. This was a real blow. I stayed in New York until January 4th. When I went back to Puerto Rico, I told my father off. I blamed him for my mother's death. You know, I can't understand her death. She died of cirrhosis of the liver. I can't remember her drinking. What I understand is that cirrhosis of the liver comes from drinking. With him I could have understood it. I would hear him come home drunk, stoned so many nights.

"My mother gave me a lot of love. We used to have our little talks. She was sick for seven years before she died. There was a cholesterol buildup. Her eyes were yellow, her face was yellow. It was terrible. She was in pain. She was that thin. She was really gone. The truth of the matter, I was glad for her when she died. At first they told her she had six months to live. She lasted seven years. I wasn't aware of all that, though. I became aware of it after her death. I finally found out what the deal was.

"After my mother died, my step-father told us: 'You have a choice, you can go to boarding school or you can go to Puerto Rico and live with your real father.' I decided from my early boarding school experience that I couldn't take that over again so I decided to go to Puerto Rico. My sister chose boarding school. They put her somewhere in Plattsburg and my brother was already going to college at Iowa State by then. They went their separate ways. I packed up my few things and left.

"I had been very close to my sister, I never cared about my brother. Anything could have happened to him, I couldn't have cared less. We were always separated. I started writing to him when I was in Leavenworth [after Dix] and I would write him and tell him the way I felt. Since that time we have started to be closer.

"After my mother died I went to Puerto Rico. It was great in the beginning. I went to three different schools. Two of them were public schools and one of them was a semi-private. The semi-private was the one I quit. I had a fight with my education teacher, me and my friend, a very close friend (he died in Vietnam) and they suspended us, but I never went back. I just quit.

"I started selling clothes in my father's store. I would save up my salary to go to New York in the summer, to be with my sister.

"I was using drugs in Puerto Rico after my mother died. I came in every day at lunch. I'd borrow ten dollars from the cashier. In Puerto Rico the bags were three dollars apiece. So I'd take nine dollars, go downstairs to the cop-man, get high, come back and be nice all day in the store selling clothes. I'd save a bag for later on in the nighttime. This kept going until my father started to get hip to the fact that something was wrong because he told the cashier not to lend me any more money. So I went through the money I had saved. I went broke; no one would lend me money.

"I finally told my father: 'I'm strung out, man I'm sick. I'm on drugs. I need ten dollars.' He wouldn't give me any. Instead he offered to take me to a doctor and get me some private treatment. I was willing to do anything. I wanted to kick, but I didn't want to go through the symptoms. So, he took me to this doctor. The doctor gave me some Librium intravenously. He gave me a bottle of Librium 100's as well, pills. So I went home to kick. I figure I ain't gonna feel nothing. It's true I didn't feel anything. I was out cold. They came and gave me the Librium intravenously. Two or three days went by. I came down with hepatitis.

"After a while I wanted to get out and walk, stretch my legs, I'd been in this bed for so long. I wanted to get high. So I looked around and wondered what could I get high with. I didn't want to shoot up, because I knew that was no good. I looked at the bottle of Librium. I took two and some coffee. That was nice. I went up the block. I didn't tell my father. Later he said: 'They say you're using drugs again.' I said: 'No, I haven't been out of bed.' He believed me.

"I went back to New York. The first day there I had eighty dollars in my pocket, I had a watch, I had one of these Cuban chains that my aunt had given me, and I had a ring. I found a junkie on the street. I said: 'Look, I wanna cop half a load.' I put two with this other guy, and I overdosed, you see. I woke up, I had no money—a walking OD, I went downstairs, I kept on walking. Luckily for me I fell down right in front of my cousin's house. When I woke up, I was inside and the first thing I did was reach for my pocket, my money. No money, no watch, no chain, no dope. Four or five days later, the hepatitis symptoms started again.

"My family was very upset. We had arguments. My brother would beg me to stop the drugs. I would say: 'Mind your business. You're married. Stay with your wife.' This is the kind of relationship we had. I would tell my sister: 'Yeah, I'm going to kick. Don't worry about it, Sis.' Anyway, even though I had hepatitis, I wouldn't go to the hospital, I didn't even want to kick the habit anymore. I guess that's the main thing, you don't want to go through the symptoms. I got really sick. I couldn't walk. I fell every time I moved. My liver would crash against my ribcage. I wouldn't go to the hospital. My eyes were yellow.

One day I was lying in my aunt's apartment, and I heard someone knocking at the door. There's my step-father. He says: 'Come on, let's go.' I asked: 'What are you talking about?' He insisted, 'You're going to the hospital.' He had a baseball bat with him. I told him: 'No, man, I ain't going to no hospital.' He says: 'I'll tell you what, you're going to that hospital for hepatitis, or I'm going to put you there.'

"He brought me over to St. Luke's. The same doctor that had treated my mother treated me. So I kicked the habit again. I got rid of the hepatitis. I came out of the hospital in thirty days. I came out pretty healthy. I went back to the same old bag. I had a close call. My friend and I were up on the roof [in New York]. We were cooking up this high. He was arguing with me. He complained that he couldn't get high from my works. We were so deep in this argument that we forgot to look downstairs. Something told me to turn around and look, and when I did I looked right into 'the man's' face. Boom! I got up and ran. I hit the door. The door wouldn't open. I came from behind and pushed. My friend lost a shoe, running away, but we got away. This was on Fourth Street. We got through the yards, came out on Third Street. Finally, we got to his house through the back door. He told me: 'Wait here, my father's home.' I had ripped my pants in the back, I was a mess. I had been thrown out of my house too. They didn't want me. I decided I'm going to have to go to Puerto Rico and get away from this. I called up my father in Puerto Rico the same day. I told him I'm going to come. He said: 'Are you using drugs?' I said: 'No, I just came out of the hospital.' So he said: 'Okay.' So I went to Puerto Rico. It was then that I decided to enlist.

"I am the only one in the family who has ever been in the Army, besides my grandfather. He enjoyed it. It was the thing to do [the Second World War and Korea]. He's an old-timer. I believe he was in the First World War too. My father tried to get into the service when he was young, but he couldn't because he had bad knees. He felt very disappointed. This was a bad shock for him. He was so pro-Army and the Army rejected him.

"The reason why I enlisted was that I wanted to get away from drugs. I was there in Puerto Rico, with my very close friend, Hector Lugo Moheco. They said we look like twins. They took us for brothers. We were both using drugs again.

"So I enlisted at Fort Brook, San Juan, Puerto Rico. I talked my friend into coming too. I was just turning eighteen. My friend was three years older. He had taken the exams and failed. So I talked him into taking the exams again. I said: 'Let's get away from this.' He said: 'No.' I said: 'Come on, let's get away from this. I'll tell you what, man, we'll go to Nam. They've got some good drugs there,' so you see, I was trying very hard to get him to enlist. He said, 'Okay,' took the exams and passed. The thing is I got rejected. I had syphilis. He went into the war. He went airborne. He did everything. Totally engrossed, he was off drugs. He died in Nam

"I finally got my shots and got rid of the syphilis. I joined up. I was really eager. I had turned eighteen. That was in '67. I was one of the fortunate ones. I got four days leave. That was beautiful, four days leave to start with. We finally left. We came to Fort Jackson. Hair gone, fitted for fatigues—the garbage they give you.

"I took Basic in Gordon. I did all right on Basic, but I wasn't the company's star pupil. They'd jump on me because they thought I was messing up—I would go to the PX, buy beer and come back drunk. I had a Christmas leave. I came home on the 4th of December, I went back on the 2nd of January. I got together with my family. They took my picture in my uniform. I really wasn't into that. But to satisfy them, I let them take pictures. I went to visit my girlfriend. We had a nice time together. Right after that we broke up. It wasn't a Dear John letter. It was a phone call. Today's age, you know, no more letters.

"I went back into the Army and finished Basic. I was shot into an AIT [training program]. They sent me to a wiring school, Fort Jackson, about January 15th or 16th. I became squad leader. I didn't mind the Army at all. I stayed there about four weeks. I was doing pretty well and they transferred me to a more advanced course, which was pole lining, in signal school. I went back to Fort Gordon, Georgia, then I started to get into a hassle. We put up the telephone poles and ran cables. I used to do my job very quickly and then watch the others. But this guy, who had graduated from the course, was our instructor. He had no rank. He was an E2 and I was E1, so he wanted to enforce his authority. He came up to me while I'm watching the others and told me to do something. I explained to him that I did my job, and like everybody else, when I was finished I sat down and watched the others. He got nasty. I called him a 'motherfucker.' He told me I could get court-martialed for that. He told me to report to the sergeant. The sergeant was an E7. I went to him, I explained what the deal was. He got nasty. "Go ahead, make a six by six," a hole. Six down, six wide, wow! No hassle.

I went out and got a shovel and dug this six by six by six. I finished. He told me to empty all the garbage cans, throw them in there and bury them up again. Okay. The next day I had blisters all over my hand. So I went back on the field. This guy, the same instructor, maybe it was a racial thing, he told me to dig out an anchor. [An anchor is six feet under ground, it holds a corner.] I told him: 'Look at my blisters.' He told me: 'Do you have a medical excuse?' I answered: 'No, but I can't do it.' He said, 'If you can't do it, you are not exempt from it . . . you have to do it.' I had an argument with him and he told me to go back to the Sergeant. The Sergeant got belligerent. We exchanged hot words. He wanted to give me an Article Fifteen . . . take my money away. I said: 'No, if they want to give me an Article Fifteen, let it be for something that I've done.' So I went AWOL, my first AWOL."

While in Segregation awaiting his trial, Carlos wrote an anguished letter to members of the Workers Defense League:

"I may be court-martialed like many others and it is so important that my story pierce the ears of the people in the world outside the stockade. . . .

"If you think that torture is no longer used you are wrong.

". . . let me give you a few cases. I'll start with Jimmy Friend (of course that is not his real name because I don't have permission to use it). I was in Mental Hygiene when I looked out the window and saw this prisoner being taken into Segregation. He was being hit on top of the head when all of a sudden he let one go that landed on Sergeant Branhover's face. [Sergeant Branhover is a lifer.] Then they really put it to him. The word from Major Casey was, 'Drop him.'

"As I was going to my cell I saw big bruisers go in his cell. He was in the straps about five or six hours. He was laid on a bunch of boards about eight inches off the ground and every thirty minutes or so he was picked up and let fall, hitting his head and abdomen, each time from higher up. As a result, after he was unstrapped the man was unable to use his legs without support, his face was bashed up and he couldn't use his arms . . . He was in cell 12 and I was in 14. The next day he was processed out of the pound.

"I was not in the same cell block at the time as this reported incident to another prisoner which took place on June 5th. His name is Johnny Sanchez and he had been to Vietnam and risked his life fighting Communism for all the Noble Reasons the government produces. The man went through hell as anyone

125

who has been to Vietnam knows. When he finally came stateside the man was a complete nervous wreck. I myself once was startled as I walked past his cell to see him there shaking. . . . Anyway, he was beat up by four guards, taken to the barber shop and all his hair was cut off. I think the Army was afraid of a protest against the treatment and conditions in the stockade and they were making an example of Johnny Sanchez of what they could do to anyone who objected or protested. They were saying that if anyone gets out of hand they would get what Johnny got. And by getting out of hand they meant being at the right place at the wrong time, and a smile when it's not supposed to be there. Anything as simple as that. . . .

"A third case, Jones, which is his real name, was told by one guard in control, 'Don't smile.' A few minutes later a smile came on his lips and all of a sudden four guards, as if anticipating his smile, came from everywhere. They pounced on this man. When the officers saw what was happening they did nothing but pass on by. When they sent him to the hospital his face was hardly visible alongside the bumps and blood. He was brought back to segregation at night so no one could see. Outcome, the man was put on Code II [very dangerous] which means shower and shave once a week only. The report when taken to the hospital was 'Necessary Force Needed and Used.'

"For the fourth case I can use the person's name because it happened to me, Carlos Rodriguez. Now I've been in segregation approximately thirty-five days, if you don't count the few hours I spent outside on June 5th, then I've been here fifty days. On July 8th, I was told to move from Cell Block 77 to Cell Block 85. After some hassle about a footlocker a gung-ho Pfc. Cleland threw my clothes on the floor. I refused to move until someone picked up my clothes and put them back where they belonged. Then Sergeant Hindman called me a punk. Spec. 4 Miller tried to beat me but I noticed him coming and ran towards the wall. Sergeant Hindman put his hands on me and I tried to protect myself. Spec. 4 Miller started punching. Next thing I knew six guards are trying to put me down. Blows on my head, punches all over but I cover my face . . . They get me down and tie my hands behind my back and begin to put the pressure on. More punches on my back, sides, head and, next thing I know Sergeant Hindman puts my head on the floor left side up, and leaves an imprint of his boot on my cheek and a bump on the other side. They kicked me in the back of my head and put a a foot on the back of my neck and applied pressure. All this after they had put my hands behind me and tied them and I was completely subdued. Later when they started walking me to the cell they tried to throw me against the edge of a building, but missed. When coming into my cell they punched me, and another prisoner saw them. They tried to put me against the bars of my door, but I side stepped. For that I got another imprint on my left side . . ."

On December 24, 1968, Captain Paul A. Buttenwieser, the resident psychologist, wrote a report on Carlos:

> This individual requires an intensive retraining in order to find means of gratification other than drugs . . . virtually impossible within the Army . . . strongly recommend discharge. It is not to be expected that further confinement would have a beneficial effect on the prisoner's personality. It is reasonable to assume that the longer his rehabilitation is postponed the less likely he is to make any improvement.

Despite this report on Carlos early in his stay at Dix he spent most of the time in the strictest confinement.

Carlos remembers his time in Fort Dix as one long nightmare: "The first time I arrived at Fort Dix was on May 8, 1968. I had gone AWOL and got caught for burglary, trying to support my heroin habit. First I was taken to the Brooklyn House of Detention for adolescents, then to Rikers Island. When I came out on bail, the MPs picked me up and took me to Fort Dix. I was only eighteen. I got into Fort Dix in the morning, and I was admitted into the stockade process. You know how the Army is, everything is hurry up and wait.

"They kept me in a bull pen. This bull pen was in the stockade itself. It's all the way in the back. I was taken into a sally port, stood on a yellow line—until the guard came in and picked me up. He took me through a gate. Then he walked me into a compound cell, past the cell blocks, past another gate, and sat me down in the bull pen.

"There were about fifteen of us sitting on an uncomfortable wooden bench with our legs dangling. As long as my legs are they couldn't reach the floor. The whole process is one person at a time. Oh, man, the typing is click with one finger. Everybody has to wait until everybody is done. If you are not finished the first night, you stay there until two o'clock in the morning. You go to sleep. They finally give you mattresses; five o'clock in the morning get up. You get only three hours sleep.

Sometimes you don't even get that much. You don't fall asleep right away. So it's an average of two or three hours sleep right away. The next morning you go through the same old monotonous routine. Tic-tac typing. So finally I got through. I stayed in Cell Block 82 for a while. Then, they transferred me into 81.

"My first trouble in 81 came when this guard wanted to put me on a detail, I had worked the night before. If you work at night, you don't have to do anything in the morning. So, OK, I worked that night and the next day they wanted to put me on KP again. I said, 'wait a minute'—I explained it to them. They said, 'Well you are not on this form,' some form that they had. 'Go to KP.' So I said, 'No, let me talk to somebody.' So they sent me to this Sergeant in B compound and I explained to him what had happened. He tells me that if a guard tells me to do some work, I am going to do the work. I said, 'No I ain't.' I got belligerent too. We both exchanged words. He got up and pushed everything off his desk, and snatched me, 'Motherfucker, if I tell you to do something, I want you to do it.' So at that time everything went through my head. I said, 'Wait a minute man.' I let it slide and told him, 'No I am not going to do anything. I did my work and that's it, man.'

"They put me in Segregation. I had about seven days DS in Cell Block 71. It has fourteen cells inside, seven cells when you walk in on the right side of the cell block, seven cells had the mesh. I was released and put in Cell Block 83. Everything was smooth there, so I made parole. From 83, I went to 65. When I was in 65, we were told that all parolees who were there at this time would be given a chance to go home for Christmas or for New Year's. Towards Christmas, people started leaving, the parolees started leaving. But we were still left on the 24th of December and we were given KP. There were only thirteen of us. So they sent small groups of us to each mess hall. While we were gone, the MPs had a meeting. Our MP told us that he had tried his best to have us released but for some reason they had a hold on us and we couldn't go. He said: 'Don't escape, don't breach parole because you will be hurting yourselves.' We went back to the mess hall. They were serving lunch. It was about twelve-thirty when this car pulled up and one by one we walked out of the mess hall and we all breached parole. We left both mess halls empty. We went to New York.

"We hit the Bronx, in fatigues, field jackets and boots. But we got away. I stayed away for about three months. At this point all I wanted was a discharge. I didn't want anything more to do with the Army, I just wanted to get out. I got arrested for loitering. My cousin turned me in. Some people say your family is your worst enemy. It was true with me. I got arrested for loitering with the intent to use narcotics. I went to court. I was still a young kid. You had to give your address at the police station, so that they could notify your family of your whereabouts, if you are a minor under twenty-one. So I just figured I might as well go ahead. They were going to find out anyway. So, I told them, I was in the Army. They took me back to Fort Dix.

"It was a year later, March, 1969. I went in there, nothing had changed. The same processing, the same hassle. This time I got put in Cell Block 83, in C compound. I spent most of the time in Seg before the riot.

"I finally got out of Seg and got a job in the dispensary with my cousin Coco. One day, I went to the barber shop, I needed a trim. My friend Zigi would always trim my hair; so I went to this chair, sat down and he trimmed my hair. This young guy came in. He talked about how he's sick. You could see through him. He was not sick. He was just trying to get out. All this does is hurt the other men, who are really sick, *so* shallow. He told Zigi he needed a haircut quickly because he wanted to go to the hospital. So, I told Zigi I'd take care of it, I'd give him a haircut. A guard saw me. He came screaming: 'You are not an authorized barber.' I said: 'Well you show me someone here who is an authorized or licensed barber. We are all prisoners.' He said: 'OK, give me your name.' So I gave him my name. I went back to my cell block; they picked me up—back to Seg. I went downstairs, into Administrative Segregation then back to D.S. During this time, I attempted suicide.

"I was in my cell, on D.S. I had stomach pains. I was just lying on my side. I had cramps. Most likely the cramps were from the D.S. chow. I asked to go on an emergency sick call, because of these cramps. They came; they handcuffed me and sent me up. Every prisoner, they handcuffed with their hands in the front, it's easier both for him and the guards. But they handcuffed me with my hands behind my back. If my hands had been down, it wouldn't have been so bad, but they had my wrists up. I had to sit down bent over. This was all harassment. There was really no reason for it. This was a pig of a guard. All through the trip he was the Pig of pigs. They took me to the hospital and signed me in. Told me to sit down. I sat down. I told him nicely: 'I am not going to be belligerent.'

CARLOS: Why don't you take the handcuffs off, put them in front or just put my wrists down, if you think I'm that violent.

GUARD: No.

CARLOS: Why, man? Why do you do this? I ain't giving you no hassle.

GUARD: I don't want you to. I want you to stay like that.

[I lay there. After a while I spoke.]

CARLOS: Look here, man, I got to go to the bathroom.

GUARD: You can't go to the bathroom. I don't want you to.

CARLOS: I have to go, man. I am going to go.

GUARD: You can't go, there is someone using it.

CARLOS: Who is using it?

GUARD: Me.

[That's the kind of guy he was. I was getting really mad inside. I stood up.]

CARLOS: Look, man, I am going to go anyway.

GUARD: If you do, I'll stop you.

[I just got up, made a move. He jumped up and grabbed me by the neck. I was handcuffed, what could I do?]

"This was in the hospital. All these people were looking at me. I guess he felt proud. Finally, they called me. They told me there was nothing wrong with me, just some cramps. They gave me a pill. I couldn't get them to change my handcuffs. They said they didn't have any authority for things like that. The guard drove me back. He took me to a duty officer. He wrote up a 508 note on me and the way I acted. I said: 'Look, sir, the way he treated me was unnecessary, the handcuffs, the wrists up . . .' The duty officer seemed to have understood, only he put his hat on and he left. He didn't talk to anybody about it. Then the guard in the small bull pen who was in control writing up the 508 said: 'We haven't searched him, have we?' Now remember, I've been in the hospital all handcuffed. I said: 'You don't have to search me, man.' 'Yeah, we have to search you,' they said. They took the handcuffs off. 'Put your hands up on the wall, spread your legs.' They kicked out my legs from under me. 'We ain't finished, put your hands back up.' I put my hands back up, they kicked my legs out. Nice, heh—back up—boom. I said: 'Look man, if you have something against me, why don't you get it off by yourselves, I am willing to take the extra time. But if you want to do something with me, let's go back here.' 'Put yours up again Rodriguez.' 'Yeah, OK.' Buck again. I'm mad. There are tears in my eyes. I just looked at them, there are three of them, laughing and enjoying it.

"I remember Rosenfield, he was the one who was driving the truck. And he didn't have any business there. But he was in there just for the fun of it. So I'm going off for the fifth time. I'm mad. I don't want to put my hands up now. They wrote on the 508 that I refused to put my hands up any longer, and also that I refused to be searched. They took me back downstairs. I had tears in my eyes and I was really mad. They put me into maximum security area. I told some Italian guard to lock me up, I told him I didn't want to harm anybody. He smiled: 'Go to your cell block.' I went to my cell block, you know, shower and shave. They gave me my razor blade, put it in my razor, tightened it up, I turned around, I took it apart, saw the razor blade, and said the hell with everything and slashed my wrists; it was May 25, 1969. I don't remember the rest. What follows was told to me by the guards: I ran to the corner with the razor blade, said: 'Come on in—my blood is pouring out.' They rushed in, the razor blade flew to the floor somewhere, I fell down—they bandaged my wrists. They got the ambulance, took me to the hospital, sewed me up. Twenty-seven stitches. They got me back to my cell.

"They had a social worker visit me, a Captain Herrick. He asked me: 'Why did you do it?' 'If I knew why I did it, I wouldn't have done it.' They don't want to hear what really happened. If they do know about it, they want to conceal it. They tell you it was just a hallucination. I told them a million times. They don't want to hear about the handcuff business. He asked me: 'Why?' I say: 'I don't know why.' 'You're shamming.' That's the way he talked, you know 'sham.' I figured, damn, I cut my wrists, and after all the loss of blood, they continued the rabbit food diet right up to June 5th."

As of this year, 1973, the five young men are free, though Tom Catlow's case is still pending. They all finished their sentences in Leavenworth, Carlos Rodriguez Torres doing the longest stint.

Jeffrey Russell is reunited with Kathy and Jeff Junior. Thanks to Mr. Vladeck he got an immediate job with the Group Health Insurance. He has taken various other jobs and at the moment is in California. He hopes to finish his college education as soon as financially possible but it was his treatment by the Army that radicalized him, his wife, Kathy, and their friends—the way no radical college professor or reading of, say, Marcuse could hope to.

Despite his acquittal, Terry Klug spent additional time in Leavenworth to serve out his original AWOL sentence. Since being released he has worked full time for the American Servicemen's Union at their national office in New York City as the Union's national organizer. Much of his time is spent traveling to ASU chapters and helping defendants in political trials such as the case of the Camp McCoy 3. Recently he has been working with veterans' problems as well. On April 18, 1971, he married Susan Lynn Steinman who works for the New York Telephone Company and is also a political activist.

The heartening development in Tom Catlow's story is that he has grown tremendously, from a devil-may-care delinquent to a deeply caring human being; not thanks to the Army's punishing brutalities but thanks to the civilians who took an interest in him, thanks in part to the Workers Defense League and most especially to his relationship with Clariss Ritter. He has developed an awareness that something can be done about the living conditions under which he suffered as a child; that there are selfless, devoted people who are working to help others change conditions and that he in turn can help. At the moment Tom is working on a book about Army deserters. He and Clariss are the parents of a one-year-old daughter, Danika.

When Tom turned himself in voluntarily for his last stint in Leavenworth, he granted a press interview in October 1971 in which beside describing his own cruel treatment in the stockade and the suit that stockade prisoners were attempting to bring against the commander of the stockade, he spoke about the whole problem of deserters:

"The military holds AWOL or desertion as the worst of crimes . . . A guy who goes AWOL for a year will do a year in a stockade or a Federal penitentiary. (They call it the disciplinary barracks at Leavenworth.) A guy who is convicted of rape may only do six months. A murderer can do a year or six months in an Army jail, whereas a guy who has refused to murder does longer. Calley did two days in the stockade. I know guys who refused to go to Vietnam because they didn't want to do what Calley did and they have done two years, three years in a military prison. Where's the justice?

"The government acknowledges that in 1969 there were 56,000 deserters in the Army, a total of 73,000 deserters in the combined services. In '69 there were 162,000 AWOLs plus 217,-000 from the Marines. In '70, 228,000 AWOLs and 89,000 deserters. At this time in '71 one out of every eight men in the service go AWOL or desert."

Bill Brakefield, the pacifist poet, had the roughest experiences in Leavenworth. After he was finally released, Bill started working as an orderly in hospitals and with sick children. He traveled to England to visit his brother and hitched the United States. More recently he is living with his sister and brother-in-law in Los Angeles. He won first place in a speech contest at UCLA and is going to Los Angeles City College majoring in Psychology. He has completed forty recent poems which his City College teacher would like to see published but Bill wants to wait and rework them. He is also doing very interesting drawings and art work.

Carlos Rodriguez Torres, who had the longest sentence, is also finally out and off parole. When Carlos was in the Fort Dix Stockade, his lawyer, Hank DiSuvero, realized that Carlos had no visitors and asked a recently divorced female acquaintance of his, Mirta Gonzales, if she would be willing to visit Carlos. Mirta, a member of the Puerto Rican Lords did. Now Carlos and Mirta are married and Carlos is a very fond stepfather of Mirta's eight-year-old daughter. Carlos is going to the Staten Island Community College and getting A's.

It is a testimony to the five young men and to their supporters that they have come back to civilian life as positively as they have, that each of them is struggling to contribute something useful to a larger community in terms of his conscience.

But the scars are there—should you talk to Bill or Jeff, Terry, Carlos or Tom, you would find an unrelenting bitterness in him toward our American society which allows itself to torture its own citizens and treat human beings as less than beasts in the name of officialdom and justice.

STOCKADE FENCE

WORLD WAR II WOODEN BARRACKS

LEFT TO RIGHT: TOM CATLOW, TERRY KLUG, JEFF RUSSELL
AND BILL BRAKEFIELD

CARLOS RODRIGUEZ TORRES BETWEEN GUARDS

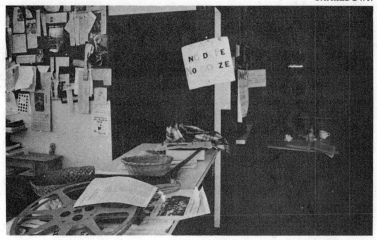

INSIDE THE COFFEEHOUSE

THE TIME HAS COME FOR A LONG-NEEDED

SHAKEDOWN

Vol. 1, No. 4   P.O. Box 68, Wrightstown, N.J.   June 6, 1969

This paper is written and published by a group of Ft. Dix GI's who in doing so have freed their minds from the involuntary servitude of the military machine. This is our "Ultimate Weapon."

STOCKADE REVOLT

The miserable conditions under which G.I.s are forced to live in the stockade at Fort Dix have caused the structure to be referred to as the "pound" -- it's only fit for a dog. Past incidents have successfully been blacked out by the brass. But they keep happening. Like most stockades around the country lately, the Pound is severely overcrowded. Most guys are there for being AWOL. The food is awful; the sanitation poor, and tensions are continually building.

The latest incident was touched off in the mess hall. The prisoners are usually served water with supper -- like dogs, their water comes in bowls. When there were enough bowls for only half the prisoners at mess on June 5, one man, named Chabot, went up and requested a bowl when he saw them come out of the dishwasher. Others followed him in this unheard-of act, also requesting bowls.

That night, word came back to the occupants of "A"

compound that Chabot had been put in "segregation"-- which is solitary confinement, Army style -- and had been charged with incitement to riot. The guys in Cell-block 67, part of A Compound, began to tear the place up. Mattresses were set on fire, and furniture was tossed out of the barracks. The action spread to cell-block 66 and then over to cell-block 84, where the guys really tore the place apart. There's hardly a single window left there. As the fire trucks roared up, trainees also arrived, with fixed bayonets, in order to restore normal "servitude." Major Casey ordered the men to return to the barracks; slowly and grudgingly, they complied.

Stockade guards put a "deadlock" on Chabot's cell because they were afraid that many prisoners were going to liberate him from his unjust confinement to seg.

It is important for all G.I.s on the base to begin to make the struggle in the stockade their struggle too. If we are going to build a movement of G.I.s, we must support our brothers in the stockade and never forget that "AN INJURY TO ONE IS AN INJURY TO ALL."

AFTERMATH OF THE RIOT

THE DEMONSTRATION MARCHES THROUGH
WRIGHTSTOWN

ON TO THE BASE

TRYING TO REASON WITH GUNS

CONFRONTATION

OUT FOR THE KILL

Fort Dix Sergeant Is Charged
In Death of Recruit After Hike

FORT DIX, N. J., Feb. 2 (AP)—The Army announced today that charges of mistreatment had been brought against a staff sergeant in connection with the death of a private who was undergoing basic training.

Tre Army said the charges against the sergeant, John D. Layton, 34 years old, of Enfield, Conn., will be thoroughly investigated to determine their truth and if they warrant a trial.

The charges were made by First Lieut. Francis T. Drury, the Army said, after the death of Pvt. John Ostergren, 22, of Norwood, Mass., on Jan. 15. Lieutenant Drury is Sergeant Layton's company commander.

Private Ostergren was pronounced dead on arrival at Walson Army Hospital here about a half hour after he was stricken midway through a scheduled five-mile training march.

Detailed Autopsy Made

The Army also announced today that "an extensive detailed" autopsy could not establish cause of death.

"The patient probably expired from a disturbance of the conducting system of the heart but this is speculation and cannot be proven by autopsy," the Army said in a statement.

Last week Representative Edwin D. Eshleman, Republican of Pennsylvania, investigated Private Ostergren's death after a soldier from his Congressional District charged that someone had ordered Private Ostergren to be physically abused.

The winning New Jersey daily lottery number yesterday was: **06729**

Tickets matching the number win $2,500. Tickets with the five numbers in reverse win $225. Tickets with the first or last four numbers in order win $225. Tickets with the first, middle or last three numbers in sequence win $25. Tickets with all five numbers scrambled win $25. Tickets matching the first and second digits, the second and third, the third and fourth or the fourth and fifth win $2.50.

The soldier, 21, m a letter to paper, The

Private heard voi walk over Private Os der said h one kick wise harm

After a Mr. Eshle await offi the case draw any

Sergean clined cor of Compan Second Ba Brigade, a

In its Army said preliminar the circui the death

"The i that Oste ers had f and at th ed by oth preliminar cated tha given to (apparent tain actic and rem made whi ferral of (

The co tion that equivalen vestigatic man said

Train

A 22-y survey te facilities sion of road wa struck l morning near the in the Br Highbrid the victi ner of 3432 Irwin Avenue, the Bronx.

DO NOT FORGET THE NEEDIEST!

Dix Sergeant
Acquitted in
Abuse Case

By FRANK McKEOWN
Staff Correspondent of THE NEWS

Fort Dix, N.J., May 14—A court of five Army officers took only 45 minutes today to determine that a drill instructor was not guilty of having kicked and verbally abused a recruit on a five-mile training march.

Those charges were brought against the DI, Staff Sgt. John D. Layton, 34, of Enfield, Conn., soon after the death of the recruit, Pvt. John Ostergren, 22, of Norwood, Mass.

An autopsy revealed that Ostergren had died of a heart seizure Jan. 15, the day of the march, but no cause was determined for the seizure. At no time was Layton accused of having done anything that led to the recruit's death.

During the court-martial, which began Wednesday, several witnesses testified that Layton had kicked Ostergren after the trainee collapsed on the hike.

They also testified that Layton had cursed the trainee, who had fallen twice previously during the march.

Layton, a Vietnam veteran, testified Friday and denied having kicked the trainee. He said he had nudged Ostergren with his foot to urge him on.

• OBITUARY •

THE NEW YORK TIMES, THE NEWARK NEWS

DAVID FENTON/LNS

5.

PRISON CAMPS AMERICAN-STYLE

The initiative for the reform of military justice—which is to say, the dismembering of it—will no more originate in the Congressional military committees than it will in the military itself, and the accommodation of those bodies of reform will be equally painful. What progressive ideas can one hope for from a Congress which before 1969 had never in its history made a complete investigation of the military penal system?

Movement, if it comes, must come from an outraged and fearful public—outraged by the things the military has done to its young men in the name of "disciplinary necessity," fearful because of the national tolerance of injustice that can result over a long period of time.

—Robert Sherrill, *Military Justice is to Justice as Military Music is to Music*

I was told by the Captain in the presence of the Colonel, in the presence of some other brass, that there were some three hundred suicide attempts a month . . .

—Mario Biaggi, on Channel 13, January 7 and 22, 1970, reporting on his visit to the Fort Dix stockade

Today the old infamous Fort Dix stockade of 1969 is razed to the ground. A new, all cinderblock, modern stockade comprising a gross "confinement area of 11,579 square feet" has been built. There are 292 prisoners imprisoned there at this writing (fall 1973).

Buildings may change but the conditions remain. This new, spic and span, very expensive complex is said to house familiar cockroaches as well as prisoners.

The conditions remain, the brutality at Fort Dix and other military bases never lets up. Quite recently, a soldier who fell during a long march at Dix was kicked on the ground by his officer. The soldied died. The officer was exonerated of all charges.

We Americans have never accepted the German people's declaration of ignorance of Auschwitz, Belsen, Dauchau. And yet concerned Americans—newspaper editors, erudite political pundits, literary agents, history professors, editorial writers—manage to maintain a willful ignorance about our own military prison camps.

Ask an older informed American about the uprisings in U.S. stockades and brigs and the most information he or she can usually muster is, "Something went on at the Presidio." Pressed further, the answer will be: "Well, there was a peaceful sit-down strike. The prisoners refused to work." Most American citizens cannot tell you what the conditions were that caused the "mutiny." Robert Sherrill's excellent book, *Military Justice is to Justice as Military Music is to Music,* which received rave reviews, has been sparsely read.

On October 14, 1968, twenty-seven young men, prisoners in the Army stockade in San Francisco sat down and sang songs demanding to see the press. The same shameful conditions existed in the Presidio stockade as existed at Fort Dix.

120 men were imprisoned in a space meant to accommodate 88. There was one toilet for 35 prisoners. Much of the time there was no toilet paper. Clogged toilets backed up into the shower rooms so that the men wore boots when they showered to avoid the floating feces. Food was scarce and there were 54 drinking cups for the entire stockade population. Again, as in the Dix stockade, epileptics and psychotics were treated as criminals and locked in solitary cells. "One of the insane inmates best remembered by former guards was a young man they nicknamed 'Penis' because he sat around in his isolation cell all day moaning, 'I want my penis.' He played with himself, urinated on the floor and rolled in it, defecated on the floor and then smeared the excrement in his hair and over his face. He also used feces for writing and finger-painting. Some of the guards, to tease him, would climb onto the mesh roof over his cell while he was trying to sleep and would jump up and down and scream to awaken him."*

* Robert Sherrill, *Military Justice is to Justice as Military Music is to Music* (New York, Harper & Row, 1970), pp. 7-8.

The "rebellion" was created by "the atmosphere of brutality" which made the men "panicky." On occasion Marine guards had been brought in to teach the prisoners a lesson in beatings and sadism.

On October 11th a severely mentally disturbed suicidal prisoner, Richard Bunch, who had joined the Army at age 17 with his parents' waiver, was fatally shot in the back by a guard. This part of the Presidio story has yet to penetrate the American consciousness.

Neither the conditions at Fort Dix nor at the Presidio are rare instances of psychopathology in the military penal system. "In this country and overseas the Pentagon supervises 138 Army, Air Force, Navy and Marine brigs and stockades with an overflow population of fifteen thousand prisoners. [Most prisoners it must be remembered, are only guilty of the heinous crime of being AWOL; half of these prisoners are simply awaiting trial.]

"From these establishments comes an endless stream of grotesque reports: of the homosexual at the brig on Treasure Island, San Francisco, who was forced to suck on a flashlight for the amusement of the Marine Guards; of the Army officers at Fort Riley, Kansas, who panicked when they discovered one of their soldiers was only twelve years old and 'hid' him for three months in solitary confinement; of the Marines forced to strip to the waist and roll in fresh feces; of the inmate in the Great Lakes Naval Training Center brig who was punished by wrapping his throat in a wet towel, clamping a bucket over his head and making him smoke cigarettes under it until he passed out; of the three hundred suicide 'gestures' at Fort Dix in one year, and of the soldiers at Fort Dix who were sprayed with water and then pushed into wintry weather, naked, for varying lengths of time (one of them for three hours); of Fort Dix soldiers seeking conscientious-objector status discharges who were imprisoned 'for their own protection' in a special cell with known homosexuals; of the Fort Leonard Wood inmate whose body was covered with gray paint and who was made to stand at attention until the paint was dry; of the Marines at Treasure Island who, according to reports from different bases, were made to do such strenuous exercises right after eating that they threw up, after which the guards pushed their faces in the vomit and made them roll in it or (in two instances reported) made them eat it."*

* *Ibid.*, pp. 192-193.

A brief though by no means conclusive survey of uprisings in American-run military prisons conveys a sense of how widespread bestial conditions are:

June 13, 1968—Fort Jackson, South Carolina: 150 stockade prisoners rebel, protesting inhuman conditions.

July 23, 1968—Fort Bragg, North Carolina: 238 prisoners seize the stockade in protest to conditions and hold it for three days.

August 16, 1968—Danang, Vietnam: Marine and Navy prisoners rebel in a section of the brig because of inhuman conditions.

August 18, 1968—Danang, Vietnam: The entire brig erupts with all prisoners taking part. One cell block is destroyed by fire. Prisoners hold the brig for three days.

October 14, 1968—Presidio, San Francisco: Following the shotgun murder of a fellow inmate, Richard Bunch, 27 inmates hold a sitdown strike and are charged with "mutiny."

January 29, 1969—Fort Leavenworth, Texas: 2,300 GIs held in the stockade, refuse to work until conditions are improved.

March 20, 1969—Fort Jackson, South Carolina: 100 GIs hold an antiwar meeting on base. Eight men are arrested ("Fort Jackson 8"). As a result of mass civilian protest, the eight are released and charges dropped.

April 8, 1969—Camp Pendleton, California: 40 prisoners hold a sit-down strike when they find another prisoner manacled in a spread-eagle position to a fence. They force his release.

May 21, 1969—Fort Ord, California: 300 GIs rebel because of impossible living conditions in the stockade.

June 5, 1969—Fort Dix, New Jersey: 250 GIs riot. Five young men are picked as organizers and face courts-martial with sentences of up to 50 years apiece.

June 22, 1969—Fort Riley, Kansas: Stockade rebellion over brutal living conditions.

September 15, 1969—Camp Pendleton, California: 200 Marine prisoners rebel over brig conditions. Company B burns a hut down. When MPs attack them, Company C smashes windows and furniture. When MPs attack them, Company A erupts in riot. The rebellion lasts all night.

March 13, 1970—Mannheim, West Germany: 100 GIs rebel in the stockade, trashing and burning buildings.

July 3, 1970—Iwakuni, Okinawa: 32 Marine prisoners take over a section of the brig and hold it for 14 hours.

December 19, 1970—Fort Hood, Texas: Stockade prisoners rebel. Privates Kevin Harvey and John Priest are made the scapegoats, charged with destruction of government property, and assault on an officer. Charges are dropped after civilian protest on base.

October 26, 1971—Fort Gordon, Georgia: 100 prisoners rebel because a GI is denied emergency leave from the stockade to visit his wife who has suffered a miscarriage. They burn a $30,000 stockade barracks to the ground. The rebellion lasts five hours.

January 10, 1972—Camp Lejeune, North Carolina: A group of prisoners stage a sit-down strike over brig conditions. Fifteen young men are picked out as leaders and put in solitary.

With all the publicity we've had of North Vietnam prisons and of the South Vietnam tiger cages, little has surfaced in the establishment press of the infamous Long Binh Jail which the Americans run in Vietnam, where we imprison our own men. During the late President Johnson's years, the soldiers dubbed it "LBJ." Standard procedural punishment at Long Binh was to put a man in a steel conex box, six feet square and maybe eight feet high. These boxes had been used for shipping typewriters and ammunition. Usually a high opening would be cut for some air but the boxes became unbearably hot under the Vietnamese sun. Army regulations permitted temporary detainees to be held in these boxes for up to 72 hours! Joseph Remcho, staff counsel for the American Civil Liberties Union of Northern California attests, "I have heard of numerous instances in which persons were confined longer than that."

The Marines had their own equivalent to Long Binh, the Danang brig. Robert Sherrill quotes Garret Gianninoto of New York City who spent six months in the Danang brig: " 'The cells were six by eight feet. The only furniture was a square box covering one-half of a twenty-five-gallon drum—this was your toilet. The drum was taken out once a day and the stuff was burned. Some fellows who had been in other prisons' solitary confinement cells complained because they didn't have any place to go to the toilet, but I would rather not have. Those toilets got pretty awful when the temperature inside the cells got up to 130 degrees. And you had to sit on the toilet all day. That was an order. You couldn't sit or lie on the floor . . . The food was lettuce and rice and in the morning, two boxes of Kellogs cornflakes and water. Stuff like that, and in the food it was commonplace to find slugs, flies and weevils.' "*

Ibid., pp. 200-201.

139

About thirty minutes south of Hiroshima by train the U.S. maintains a brig at the Marine Corps Air Station in Iwa Kuni, Japan. Mark Amsterdam of the Center of Constitutional Rights was there and told me the same ugly story of inhuman conditions. Sentenced prisoners were combined with unsentenced prisoners and received the same treatment. Prisoners underwent the "rabbit chow" diet for months at a time. One prisoner fainted because of the starvation diet, fell and cracked his head open. He was taken to the hospital, stitched up and brought right back to his cell in segregation and put on the same starvation diet.

Another prisoner was kept in the hog-tied position, which Carlos described so vividly in his letter from Fort Dix. The prisoner's hands were shackled at the wrists, his feet shackled at the ankles and then hands and feet strapped together. He was kept in that position for over a week. The guards would come in and jump on him. Mark Amsterdam saw the scars on this young man's wrists months after the torture.

Twelve miles from the former extermination camp at Dachau, the U.S. Army runs a prison where five prisoners were severely beaten and kicked by an officer who justified his brutality with the argument that he was "only following orders." He was acquitted of any wrong doing. As Fred Cohn has pointed out in his article, "Soldiers Say No,"* no officer is sent to a stockade when accused of a crime.

Racism is rampant in the U.S. armed forces; its most bestial form is in the stockades and brigs where men can be put in solitary for merely "dapping" (military term for the black handshake of tapping the upturned palm of a friend's hand). One of the less touted facts in our history books is that the U.S. armed services were segregated as late as 1948. It took an Executive order by President Truman to desegregate the Army, Navy and Marines.

On April 5, 1972, Melvin R. Laird, then Secretary of Defense, established the "Task Force on Administration of Military Justice in the Armed Forces." On November 30, 1972 the task force came out with a four-volume report of findings. With such a strong all-embracing title one would have thought the report would deal with the brutalities in brigs and stockades; the pre-trial confinements; the administering of identical treatment to sentenced and unsentenced prisoners; the hideous, inhuman, unsanitary conditions; as well as the tremendous racial inequities in these prisons.

* Robert Lefcourt, *Law Against the People* (New York, Random House, 1971).

140

But the questions the Task Force was asked to look into were very limited:

"—To determine the nature and extent of racial discrimination in the administration of military justice,

—To assess the impact of factors contributing to disparate punishment,

—To judge the impact of racially-related practices on the administration of military justice and respect for law, and

—To recommend ways to strengthen the military justice system and 'enhance the opportunity' for equal justice for every American serviceman and woman."

The entire four volumes are devoted to the problem of racism. It concludes with what every recruitee knows, that racism is rampant in the Armed Forces and it has some good recommendations.

On February 22, 1973 Senator Birch Bayh, speaking for himself and Senators Randolph and Hart, introduced a bill to revise the Uniform Code of Military Justice.

Senator Bayh introduced his bill by saying,

> . . . I am introducing a bill today which I believe is one of the most comprehensive—and at the same time realistic and workable—plans ever proposed for the meaningful reform of our military justice system. The main thrust of this bill is an attempt to eliminate completely all danger of command influence, the possibility—or even the appearance—that the commanding officer of an accused man could affect the outcome of his court-martial. . . . As long as the remotest possibility of undue command influence remains, we will never be able to avoid the implication—or at least the appearance—of fundamental unfairness. And no such system of justice can earn or maintain the respect of those it serves.

He also made the point that, "Historically, the most far-reaching reforms of our military justice systems have come at the end of times of war. We have now reached the end of our involvement in the most protracted war in American history. Now that the fighting is over we can apply the lessons we have learned in that tragic conflict by—at the least—improving the quality of justice for those who serve our Nation in the military."

The bill is comprehensive and deals with remedying many of the horrors that took place at Fort Dix and brigs and stockades run by Americans throughout the world. That we

141

should have to amend our laws in this year of 1973 to include article 55 is a sad comment on our sad times. The Amendment reads: "Punishment by flogging, or by branding, marking, or tattooing on the body, or any other cruel or unusual punishment, may not be adjudged by any military judge or inflicted upon any person subject to this captor. The use of irons, single or double, except for the purpose of safe custody, is prohibited."

This bill was read twice in Congress and in the Senate and referred to the Committee on Armed Services. This very important bill has been held up indefinitely as two of the members of the special committee on Armed Services are tied up in other committees, Senator Ervin with the Watergate hearings and Senator Stennis deep in the hearings of the secret bombings of Laos and Cambodia.

So who knows when this bill will be passed, if ever. As Mark Amsterdam writes: "as long as prisons remain cages, removed from public inspection and scrutiny, and as long as military lawyers remain insensitive to the conditions or too busy to prepare the proper motions, the men and women behind bars may have no other recourse but to take matters into their own hands and force the public to become aware of the degrading brutal nature of prison existence." As a footnote, Amsterdam cites the young man who wrote his Congressman for help from the Iwakuni Marine brig, telling of the brutalities there. His Congressman wrote back:

". . . Of course, all this could have been avoided by you in the first instance with proper conduct on your part. I trust you will attempt to comport yourself properly in the future." L. Mendel Rivers, Chairman, Committee in Armed Services.

This book was started in June of 1969 and is being finished August 1973 in the year of our Watergate. There is a tragic connection between the riot at Fort Dix and the attitude that culminated in the breaking and entering at Watergate.

Is it any wonder that leaders who can cage, starve and brutalize their own young men who rebel against an unjust war, will commit perjury, burglary and use every dirty trick imaginable to gain their own petty ends?

AFTERWORD: THE CAGE

Bestial conditions do not begin and end behind the barbed wires of a stockade. The stockade is hell, but like other American military installations, Fort Dix has a purgatory that some soldiers consider worse than the stockade: a holding facility, an area where men are billeted, waiting to be processed either for reassignment, for discharge or for courts-martial. During a period of two years this area has been variously called "SPB," "SPD" and more recently "PCF" (Special Personnel Battalion, Special Personnel Detachment, Personnel Control Facility).

On July 25-27, 1970, there was an uprising in this area; a few chosen men were singled out as scapegoats for a massive rebellion. This time ten men, later to become known as the Fort Dix 10,* were put in the stockade accused of stealing one watch, though the uprising consisted of a total work stoppage in which the majority of the soldiers in the area took part.

The area was then called SPB. During World War II, when the troops were segregated, this is where the Black brigades were billeted. It's over a mile away from any other part of the base. Though no longer segregated, everyone knows what it was in the past. In 1970 the majority of men in SPD were black and Puerto Rican.

Often the men in the area had no hot water, no way to keep clean, no foot lockers to keep their clothes in and never enough beds to sleep in. There had been no heat in February of 1970 and on the average, February was the coldest month of the year. Nobody wore insignia or rank because the men had no uniforms. The exact number of men changed from day to day. The guess then was around one thousand and there were 54 chairs in the mess hall. SPB consisted of six platoons and each platoon had about one hundred and forty men. Some of the platoons were discharge platoons and a discharge platoon might dwindle down to zero. On the other hand, two or three busloads of returning AWOLers might arrive. Most of them were assigned to SPB.

The crime rate in SPB was so high that the post taxis were not allowed in the area. There were no phones. To make a phone call out you had to go at least a quarter of a mile. The

* Three young law students, Tim Coulter, then of the Military Law Center, Gus Reichbach of the Law Commune, and Fred Gross of the Workers Defense League, provided me with this material.

personnel in terms of staff cadre was very poor. It was a savage jungle like a ghetto with every man against every other man, and the drug traffic was rampant.

A group of black GIs started to get together to try to improve living conditions in the area. Everyone involved was a Spec. 4 or 5 with one Buck Sergeant. They started meeting regularly in April. They were determined to change things in SPD. They would get groups of men together and talk about black history, black pride and the black liberation movement. They were saying: "Let's get off each other's backs. Let's not steal from each other. Let's try and protect each other; get rid of the junkies." Summer came along and it was hot.

On Wednesday, July 22nd, all hell broke loose at SPD, robberies, beatings, a rash of assaults. Colonel Bidwell called a curfew. The Colonel personally went around the barracks enforcing the curfew. Men were picked out and sent to the stockade in what they felt was an arbitrary manner. This happened repeatedly and the men grew angry.

On the morning of Saturday, the 25th of July, members of the original black group walked around all of SPB saying, "Let's not go out on detail. It's time we did something about this place." The soldiers didn't go to work. They gathered in a rump formation outside and held a mass meeting. They decided to present their grievances to Colonel Weddell, Commanding Officer of Special Troops, and to Colonel Bidwell, who was Commander of SPB. The Colonels came and had their meeting with Sergeants Woods, Coon and Poindexter who represented the SPBers. The officers listened but offered no plan or remedy for the grievances. The meeting took place around the middle of the day. That night, at 9:00 P.M., Normandy Hall, an old wood-frame building that wasn't being used, caught fire. It was gutted. Fire trucks arrived and a big crowd gathered. All the officers came. The fire was put out. Colonel Bidwell approached Woods and Coon and said: "Well, Woods, I hope you're satisfied. I hope you're happy." Soldiers started complaining to Colonel Bidwell about the conditions. And he said: "Well, if you guys don't like it around here, just go AWOL." He called another curfew.

Monday morning an incident occurred outside the main administrative building. They had a cage inside the building that was supposedly only used for temporary detention, but apparently the week before a soldier had been kept in the cage for four days. They'd been holding soldiers in the cage for long periods of time. The men were furious about it. One of the cage guards stuck his head out the door and some soldiers grabbed him, dragged him out and beat him up. He was sent to the hospital. That night a white soldier named Rice was sleeping in the 2nd Platoon, where most of the original meetings had taken place. He was awakened and was roughed up, and in the process somebody took his watch. He claimed that he had originally found that watch in a snowbank. He complained to the officers. He had no idea who had taken the watch. But the next day, Tuesday, he saw a soldier named Collins wearing what he thought was his watch. He called out the Sergeant and the Company Commander. They grabbed Collins and sent him to the stockade and Rice got the watch back. This same Tuesday, the CID became involved in the Rice case and started taking statements from alleged witnesses.

Douglas Houston, a black soldier who was not a regular SPDer, but what they call cadre [staff], told the CID that he knew the names of the people who were causing all the trouble. He ran down a long list of people: Woods, Pettis, Coon, Prendergast, Maxwell, Hall, Witherspoon, Poindexter, Lews, on and on. He didn't say what they did. All he said was, "I believe these are the ones who are causing all the incidents that take place at SPD." No precise evidential testimony was given. However, he claimed that he saw the incident of Rice getting robbed and he said that he knew the soldier who actually took the watch and he named Collins. Whether Houston already knew about Collins being found with the watch, nobody knows. Every man named by Houston was put in the stockade on the grounds of stealing one watch.

The first session of the 32 hearings on this case convened on the 21st of August, 1970. They brought Houston in from Philly. He had been sent on leave immediately after he made his original statement. He was supposed to go through a line-up, but he just couldn't do it. He was even unable to write out a description of the people he expected to identify. He refused to testify and he refused to go to any line-ups. And that was the last the SPDers saw of Houston. After that, his statement to the CID could not be used as evidence in the pre-trial hearings. But the men he had named were still in the stockade in September, 1970. The men who got out were the ones who gave testimony to the CID.

On April 12, 1971, Larry Jackson, a reporter for the *Trentonian,* Stuart Loory, a reporter for the *Los Angeles Times*, Edwin Knoll, an editor of the *Progressive* magazine, Clariss

Ritter of the Workers' Defense League, Mike Uhal of the War Crimes Bureau, and this writer accompanied Congressman Ronald Dellums from California's seventh district on a surprise visit to the Fort Dix PCF.*

Usually a congressional investigating committee is given the Cook's tour. They see only what the Army wants them to see. They are forbidden to talk to the prisoners. They are fed a steak dinner in the mess and they leave with an impression that the radicals are exaggerating the evils of stockade conditions. Such a tour was made at Dix after the Presidio uprising when the question was raised in Congress as to whether the Presidio was just the tip of an iceberg hiding abuses in countless other Army, Marine and Air Force stockades and Navy brigs. The Dix stockade tour was made on April 17, 1969, a month and a half before the riot. Headlines in the New York Post: THE ARMY MADE TALKING TO THE PRISONERS OFF LIMITS AND THEN OPENED ITS FORT DIX STOCKADE. The Army made a travesty out of the investigation, the press dutifully reported the travesty but nobody went further and said this isn't an investigation, this is an insult to Senators, reporters and the people of America. July of 1970 congressmen flew halfway round the world to investigate conditions in Con Son and there they poked their noses into areas from which they had been barred by the American Army. They made it their business to find the "tiger cages" and to let the American people know how the South Vietnamese treated their political prisoners. But on their own soil it would seem Americans are loath to find out how we are treating our own young men.

Congressman Dellums was a new Congressman, a freshman Representative from Berkeley, possibly the first radical congressman we have had. He was active enough to have drawn the notice of Vice President Agnew who called him a "radical extremist" to which Ron Dellums replied: "If being an advocate of peace, justice and humanity towards all human beings is radical, then I'm glad to be called a radical." Vice President Agnew also accused Dellums of running for Congress to bring "the walls down" and Dellums agreed to this charge too. Congressman Dellums is six feet four, with a courteous, mellifluous voice. He insists on going through the proper channels in his investigative work but he also insists upon seeing what he wants to see.

On that warm April day in 1971, Congressman Dellums insisted that the group of investigators go through the proper

* formerly SPB

146

channels in our investigation against the wishes of some of us who felt that the Army would cover up or close off areas when they knew our purpose. First we went to the post headquarters to ask permission to examine PCF. Maj. Gen. Howard Cooksey, the post commander, was not in nor was his deputy Brigadier General Robert Haldane. We waited an hour while officers scurried up and down stairs and in and out of doors. We were told that they were trying to find out if Congressman Dellums was indeed Congressman Dellums and this took telephone calls to Washington. We were certain that the officers were checking on all of our credentials, but we suspected that at the same time other officers were probably scurrying to clean things up before we arrived at PCF. We need not have worried; all the scurrying in the world would not have cleaned up PCF.

When we got to PCF we found a shambles on the flat ordered Army grounds: World War II battered, wooden two-story buildings, broken windows, flaking paint and filth. Men lay stoned on wooden steps leading to the filthy barracks. Others stood around listlessly in the pale April sun.

Once there was a myth among our ghetto youth that the Army stood for a disciplined, ordered way of life out of the drugs and slums of our urban pigsties. In PCF men told us of eating with their fingers because there were inadequate eating utensils. Inside the barracks, we found shards of glass on the floor, beds without mattresses, clogged toilets and sinks, water six inches deep in one of the shower stalls.

We spoke with a group of Puerto Rican soldiers who could only speak Spanish, through a bilingual soldier friend of theirs, and were told that they would prefer to be in the stockade to PCF. We passed a totally gutted barracks from a recent fire. When we got to the mess hall the meal was over but we spoke to a soldier on KP duty whose arms bore needle trackings below his rolled up sleeves. "Treatment for addicts," he told us, "is a big joke around here. They tell you, 'That's your problem.'"

Many of the men in PCF were Vietnam veterans. Many of them sat up all night because of the shortage of beds. Men told us of having the boots taken off their feet while they slept, watches stolen, and wallet pockets cut away with razors. The men had no regular bunks. They got blankets and sheets for their beds only if they were willing to risk having them stolen and then having to pay $7 to replace them.

After we had talked to a variety of miserable GIs, Dellums

asked to see what several soldiers had referred to as "the cage." He assured Lieutenant Colonel John Cook, who was accompanying the tour, that he understood that the word "cage" might be a euphemism the men used but he would very much like to see the place to which they were referring.

First the group was taken to a room with one wired wall which is now used as a baggage room. This used to be called the cage, Lieutenant Colonel Cook explained. Dellums was not satisfied—he insisted that he would like to see what the men called the cage now. To our horror and shame we were taken to a cage with thirty-odd men sitting inside. The bars reached from floor to ceiling enclosing a space twenty-eight square feet inside a larger room. Outside the cage at one end some officers sat on a raised platform filling out endless forms beside motionless armed guards.

The men inside the cage sat in a state of such despair that they neither read, talked, nor looked at each other. They sat on wooden chairs. Had a film director tried to express the ignominy the men felt by the placement of these chairs he could not have done a better job than the men had themselves. When they snapped to attention at the command of Lieutenant Colonel Cook we saw that none of these men faced each other, that no inmate had to recognize in another's eyes that he, this godforsaken soldier, had sunk so low as to be caged like an animal.

We spoke through the bars to some of the closest prisoners. One young man was in a terrible state as his wife had no knowledge of his whereabouts and the officers would not let him out to phone her, nor would they get word to her.

We had to remind ourselves that this was not a stockade, that in theory these men were accused of no more heinous crime than of having returned, in many cases voluntarily, from being AWOL.

The cage was not supposed to be used punitively, but when Congressman Dellums spoke to the men inside the cage, he found one man recovering from a nervous breakdown who had asked to see the base psychiatrist but instead had been ordered on KP duty, had refused, and had been placed in the cage on Saturday. This was Monday. He was still in the cage and clearly in need of mental help. Three other men had been put in the cage because they were accused of beating another man with bunk adapters the night before and a fifth man was charged with possession of heroin and dumped in the cage.

Edwin Knoll, the oldest reporter among us, commented: "Each time I come on one of these tours I expect the worst, but it always turns out worse then I expected." Knoll wrote in the June 1971 issue of the *Progressive* magazine: "Of the conditions he [Congressman Dellums] has seen so far, nothing is in more desperate need of correction than the PCF at Fort Dix . . . The Dix PCF is a jungle where men are processed in a huge cage—sometimes for forty-eight hours or more—and then assigned to filthy ramshackle barracks built during World War II to last five years." Ron Dellum's tour of stockades included the ones in Fort Meade, Maryland; Fort Bragg, North Carolina; and Fort Leavenworth, Kansas.

At the end of the tour, after passing Normandy Hall, (still gutted from the 1970 uprising), after passing men sleeping on doorsteps, the group of investigators repaired to the Commanding General's office. As Dellums entered, a young captain stepped between the rest of the group and Dellums. The Captain closed the door in our faces. At this point Edwin Knoll showed his savvy. He gave the young captain a note to deliver to Congressman Dellums with the coffee which was being taken to the Major General and the Congressman. A minute later we were welcomed inside.

The room in which we met with the Major General was a pleasant bare office, no signs of military pomp. Major General Cooksey has an Eisenhower, grandfatherly look. His eyes are set far apart, recalling both the late General and his brother, Milton. His face shows great intelligence. He is gracious, willing to listen as well as to talk. He speaks in an unaffected American conversational tone. He is not a speechmaker, nor would one imagine him referring to young men who differed with his point of view as "punks" or "creeps" as was the habit of one stockade commander.

Major General Howard Cooksey was born in Brentsville, Virginia on June 21, 1921. He had served in the Northern Philippines and Luzon campaigns in World War II, with the seventh infantry in the Korean war, in Berlin as deputy Commander of the 6th Infantry regiment from 1961-62 and as Assistant Division Commander of the "Americal" Division in Vietnam from June, 1968 to May, 1969.

He had received the Distinguished Service Medal, Silver Star, Legion of Merit, Bronze Star Medal with two Oak Leaf Clusters, Air Medal with fourteen Oak Leaf Clusters, Army Commendation Medal with two Oak Leaf Clusters, Purple Heart,

149

RVN National Order 5th Class, RVN Gallantary Cross with Palm RVN Social Service Medal 1st Class, Combat Infantry Badge with Star, Parachutist Badge.

In January, 1970, Major General Howard Cooksey assumed command of the U.S. Army Training Center at Fort Dix, New Jersey.

That hot April afternoon, the General never raised his voice in disagreement. What appalled us was that this civilized cultured man could accept PCF conditions, cage and all, with a complacent smile. He was gently disturbed to hear that five of the cage's inmates were there for punitive reasons and told one of the officers to look into it. But he didn't seem unduly disturbed. The General's heart belonged to a new program he initiated called the "Honor Platoon," a rehabilitation group that had started for one hundred men in PCF. These men were to be given special training. The General wanted to tell us all about it but Congressman Dellums kept coming back to the conditions we visitors had just witnessed. Dellums said that he was glad there was an innovative program for those boys who were eager to rejoin the Army, but what about all those other poor souls, who live in ghastly conditions, some of whom can't even speak the language? And why is the cage there at all?

In trying to explain the existence of the cage, the Major General cited the enormous amount of paper work and the need to keep the men at hand and then he made a startling statement. "Sometimes," he said, "the FBI brings us civilians and of course they are put in the cage and have no papers at all." We wondered for a split second if this was a veiled personal threat to us all.

Three days after our tour, Larry Jackson (the first reporter to do a series of articles on the conditions in PCF which ran both in the *Trentonian* and in the *Washington Post*) had dinner with a PCF Sergeant. He was driving the Sergeant back to PCF when Larry noticed an MP car and an ambulance speeding down the street. He tried to find out what was going on. He was roughed up by the MPs.

Beyond the fact that MPs were quick to rough up a civilian reporter on PCF, which is supposed to be an "open post," this incident is interesting in the light of Larry Jackson because Larry served in Korea and was a policeman before being a reporter. He had bragged to us all that his articles were responsible for stricter measures being taken against the men in PCF—that General Cooksey was considering fencing in the whole area thanks to Larry's reporting. After his tour with Congressman Dellums and after being manhandled by the MPs, Larry was ever so slightly radicalized.

On June 6th, two months after Congressman Dellums' tour, reporter Stuart Loory returned to the PCF at Dix. He found improvements, though the Fort Dix public information office denied that Dellums' visit had anything to do with them. But after Dellums made his tour, several high-ranking Army officers paid their own visits and the results he was told were:

—A new commander, Lieutenant Colonel Howard L. Moon, an infantry combat veteran who is black.

—The removal of the locked door on the cage.

—A complete cleanup in the barracks and the provision of a bed and at least a mattress for each of the men living at the PCF.

—A start toward cutting red tape so that action against the men will be taken more quickly.

But on further inspection, Loory felt that the conditions at PCF were still miserable. Two soldiers trying to get out of the Army were doing time at PCF and told Loory that things were not so hot.

James Fowler, 21, of Dover, N.J. had been AWOL for four months and wanted to get out of the Army permanently because he claimed the Army had promised to put him in the Army Security Agency where he could learn the Thai language and then reneged on the promise, putting him in the infantry instead. Recently Fowler experienced a tough night in the barracks at PCF. First a group of his barrackmates came around his bed, awakened him and demanded to see his wallet. They wanted his money. A resourceful fellow, knowledgeable about the law-and-order problem in PCF, he had left his wallet with a buddy in another unit. The would-be holdup men moved on to another bed. Finally back to sleep, wearing a pair of fatigues marked Addison (Fowler's own had been taken from him), his boots tightly laced up around his ankles, he was awakened once more. This time it was a companymate trying to peddle some marijuana.

Fowler's buddy, Sergeant Wallace Reed, a 22 year-old veteran of Vietnam, carried his most prized possessions wherever he went, neatly tied together in a white towel: a shaving kit, a book of Zen Buddhism and a box of green writing paper. He knew (being in PCF) that if he put the bundle down, even while on a detail like policing the company area, he would risk having it stolen immediately. Sergeant Reed's father was a noncommissioned career officer who retired after twenty-two years in the Army. Sgt. Wallace Reed went AWOL from Fort Hood, Texas for fourteen months. It was the only way he could get away from the military drug culture into which he was falling. He was also turning away from the Vietnam war and now considers himself a Conscientious Objector and a pacifist. While AWOL, he married a pacifist and they have since had a child. A dog-handler in Vietnam who was sent out on missions to track the enemy, he is now so disenchanted with his military experience that he never wants his son to see him in uniform. "If I can get the right kind of discharge," he said, "I want to go back to school and learn forestry." Meanwhile Loory writes, "Fowler and Reed along with hundreds of others at Fort Dix, are caught up in an existence which, although it has improved markedly in the last two months, can best be compared to Skid Row."

Loory heard from Lieutenant Colonel Howard Moon of another fellow, a Puerto Rican young man whose story is very reminiscent of the troubles that Carlos Rodriguez Torres of the '69 riot had in the stockade:

"We had a fellow last November by the name of Orlando Lopez. He claimed he was a civilian but Army records showed there was an AWOL Orlando Lopez." The MPs in New York had picked him up, charged him with being AWOL and sent him to Dix. "It took us all afternoon to straighten it out. He was not the guy. We took up a collection to raise the $2.40 to put him on a bus back to New York."

The following cases are typical of the young men in PCF.*

Case A: A Haitian soldier who spoke little English at the time of induction. He trained as an infantryman and when he got his order to Vietnam he was forced to go AWOL because he knew he didn't speak enough English to make it through. He surrendered himself to the FBI after one year. He was placed in the Fort Dix stockade and after seven weeks in pre-trial confinement, charges were dismissed because he had been given no actual reporting date. He spent the next five weeks in PCF (then known as Special Processing Battalion) and was returned to the stockade on an AWOL charge for another year because of red-tape confusion.

He went AWOL again.

The Workers Defense League surrendered him in January

* Clariss Ritter and Fred Gross of the WDL furnished this material.

and he was immediately placed in the stockade. After two weeks he submitted a request for undesirable discharge in lieu of court-martial. The WDL spent an entire day trying to get him out of confinement but every level of authority claimed that someone else had to make that decision. They wrote Major General Cooksey on March 9, 1971 for a personal interview to get him out of the stockade, and to grant the soldier an honorable discharge to protect his citizenship status. His confinement officers agreed that he presented no discipline problem and should not be in the stockade. He had two requests in for discharge—one for erroneous induction and one for undesirable discharge.

As of this writing, the man's request for undesirable discharge has been denied. He is to be court-martialed by a court that can impose a bad conduct discharge. No one will talk to the WDL about letting him out of the stockade, nor allow them to present any mitigating evidence about his situation and why he should receive an honorable discharge in lieu of court-martial.

Case B: A Puerto Rican soldier who would probably not have been inducted had he been given adequate English comprehension tests. His first application for hardship discharge was denied because he had not been advised as to what it should contain and because it was not presented in fluent English. His First Sergeant refused to accept a second application in violation of military regulations. He was forced to go AWOL to work and support his sick wife, his own family and his wife's family in Puerto Rico. WDL surrendered him in January, went into federal court on a *mandamus* and *habeas corpus* petition. The Army conceded error and agreed to accept a new application for hardship discharge.

He was in PCF for three months without court-martial and is awaiting decision on the discharge. He has received only a $25 advance on pay. In March, his wife's military allotment did not arrive in time to pay the rent. WDL arranged with Captain Brown for him to remain one extra day on pass to talk to his wife's landlord. When he returned to PCF his first sergeant forced him to do extra duty because he had been "AWOL." He tried to explain (in his broken English) and to show the First Sergeant a letter we had written Captain Brown requesting pay, but the first sergeant told him he was nothing but a "goddam AWOL" and he didn't want to hear about Captain Brown or letters or anything. WDL wrote Captain Brown in protest. A week later this same First Sergeant called in the soldier and gave him hell for complaining. This soldier reports that most of the Puerto Rican soldiers take blankets home to their families who have no heat. (He also had his own clothes ripped off.)

Case C: A Puerto Rican soldier who could not get the Army to accept hardship discharge application so he went AWOL. He surrendered himself and was sent to PCF. He spent nine months there and was finally thrown in the stockade and charged with AWOL for those nine months because his records had been lost. Charges were eventually dismissed because there was no evidence against him, although he had evidence that he was, in fact, there. Colonel Weddell made an administrative decision that those nine months were to be considered "bad time" because no one had authorized him to remain away. One week after charges were dismissed and he was returned to PCF from the stockade, the morning report was incorrect and he was again placed in AWOL status. His first sergeant accompanied him to personnel to correct the mistake. He received pay for the next three months and then was told that since he had been AWOL for the past three months he had been dropped from the rolls and could receive no further pay. He spent over a month trying to get this straightened out before he went AWOL to work and support his wife. Although his first sergeant assured him that he had a good case and could win back all of his "lost time," he was forced to accept undesirable discharge because he would not trust the PCF. He was sure they would lose his records a third time.

Case D: A black soldier who was sent home on excess leave pending discharge from PCF about the time of the major attacks on MPs in the area "because the racial tensions were so bad at PCF that they were trying to get black men out of there." He returned to New York City and set about to get himself established. He recently received notice that he is AWOL in deserter status. Now he stands to lose everything.

Case E: A black soldier whose hardship discharge application was unlawfully denied so he was forced to go AWOL. He surrendered himself to PCF and attempted to submit a new application for hardship discharge. After several weeks, he was told that, according to regulations, he had not been gone long enough to be attached to PCF (he was AWOL for under thirty days). He would have to proceed to Oakland or Vietnam before resubmitting. He was literally forced to go AWOL for over thirty days in order not to leave the area where his family lived while the discharge application was processed. When he returned (approximately forty-two days later so that he would be dropped from the rolls at Oakland) and attempted to submit the application, he was told it was not a good idea because as soon as he was court-martialed he would be shipped out and the application might get lost. WDL submitted the application at his court-martial and the judge deferred sentencing pending final decision. HE WAS INFORMED HIS APPLICATION FOR HARD-SHIP DISCHARGE WAS APPROVED. WDL had spoken with him often about the problems at PCF, and he angrily said he wishes people would quit blaming the problems on "drugs." He reported that drug addiction is not that high (yet) because he does not believe all drug users are addicts. He said that the living conditions in PCF give rise to drug use and consequently to crime. He had not been paid for several of the weeks he spent at PCF. He reported that the men are all very demoralized by the conditions and that although they *knew* their battle lines are improperly drawn, their frustrations over living conditions prevent any constructive thought. He reported that most of the soldiers (at least in his barracks) are Vietnam veterans and that they sit up at night (because there aren't enough beds) and talk about the incidents of racism they have experienced in the Army (basic training companies in the south where the Klan regularly raided and jumped on blacks; white NCO's and officers in Vietnam who directly or indirectly tried to kill them or get them killed, etc.). He says that none of the guys really want to fight each other, but because of the racist attacks, the black and brown soldiers have experienced all their lives and because of the incredible living conditions at PCF, the only outlet for their frustrations is against the brothers of the white minority

Case F: A white soldier who turned himself in a St. Albans Naval Hospital, Queens, asked for help kicking heroin, and reported his last fix was that morning. Within two hours he was released to the Armed Forces Police Detachment, without having been psychiatrically or medically examined. He spent several hours in the 1st Precinct lock-up in Manhattan before being transferred to Fort Dix. He spent hours in the cage at PCF before he was interviewed. He told the interviewing officer he had over-extended his emergency leave from Thailand. He had a family hardship which did not meet regulatory requirements. He told the officer of his heroin addiction. The interviewing officer told him he would receive a plane ticket for immediate deployment back to Thailand. He became addicted to heroin in Thailand and spent a week in an Army hospital there for an O.D.

Case G: A white soldier whose background is one of poverty and a family of honorably discharged men: he was inducted despite medical disqualification. He went home for one weekend during Basic without pass. When he returned, nothing happened. That week he failed to pass marksmanship on the rifle range so was denied a weekend pass. He went home anyway and four days later was called in to accept Article 15. He told his commanding officer he did not feel it was fair to deny a man a pass simply because he couldn't qualify on the range. That weekend he went home again without a pass and on Monday his commanding officer had the MPs come and take him to PCF. He spent one night there and split. "It's simple. I won't go back to that place. It's a pigsty and no one should have to live like that."

These cases could be multiplied many times over. The overwhelming majority of men at PCF are men who are entitled to discharge. Most of them are forced to go AWOL in order to get help for their problems, i.e., family hardship, personal, medical, or psychiatric, drug addiction, inability to communicate in English. Many men go AWOL in order to qualify for undesirable discharge. But even these men, when talked to, provide information on some disqualifying factor which should exempt them from military service. Almost none of the men would be there except for illegal conscription. Many, like Tom Catlow, have been given the choice of enlisting or going to jail for civilian offenses, some even before they are brought to trial.

Most of the men at PCF will be coming out of the Army with undesirable, bad conduct or dishonorable discharges. When they hit the streets there will be virtually nowhere for them to go but back to the ghetto. Veterans with U.D.'s have no veteran's benefits—not even the right to get N.Y. State unemployment insurance—and they can't get jobs.

According to a soldier in PCF, four men had died in SPD. Three of them died in the fall and one in the spring and the soldier said he personally knew two of the men. One died as a result of a fight and he believed that the fight involved the question of beds. The other died of an overdose. There were rumors of two other deaths.

On that memorable afternoon of April, 1971, when Major General Cooksey was outlining the need for the cage, one of his explanations was that this way the men were available for appointments with, say, the Health Department or other agencies. As he was giving this explanation, our thoughts went to the case history of an epileptic, the last case history that Fred Gross had told us about:

"I have a counselee who is an epileptic and who is in and out of PCF. He'd get tired of waiting for them to do something and he'd split. We finally have his discharge on the way and he's now on leave. His name is Jean Paul Voyette. The last time he left, he left without realizing that he was being processed for his psychiatric out. He had had a term in SPD at Fort Meade; a term in PCF at Fort Dix, and he would wait, three, four and eight weeks for an action and no action would come. He felt that he was not getting medical attention for his epilepsy. At Walter Reed Hospital they had diagnosed him as having idiopathic epilepsy which means an epilepsy which is unique to the individual. As such they could claim that it did not fall within discharge regulations.

"When he came to me, I said, 'Look, it's going to take time. All I can do is assure you that I am going to pull every string that I possibly can!' Despite my efforts, the Army managed the standard snafus. When he was turned in PCF at Dix I immediately went to the Walson Hospital's special inquiries division which is prepared to handle lawyers, mothers, doctors on any medical problem. I described the situation and I asked that we have a psychiatric appointment and that he have a neurological examination. I delivered the order for him to have his examination the following morning by hand to PCF. Despite this there was a snafu. He didn't get the examination.

"The first or second night after Voyette returned to PCF, he went to the NCO and said, 'I'm about to have an epileptic seizure.' He was sent over to Walson Hospital. The Doctor on duty at the hospital gave him a Dilantin, which is a standard anti-convulsive and a phenobarbital which is a barbiturate with mild anti-convulsive capability. Johnny's experience had been that these were inadequate and he told that to the doctor. The doctor said, 'You go back to your unit. I'm the doctor.' He went back to his unit in SPD. An hour later he had a seizure in the bathroom. I don't know if Dilantin would take effect within an hour, so that there may not be any malpractice involved, but it was terrifying for the fellow who was in the bathroom with him.

"The first night that Johnny got back they put him in the cage. They didn't get him processed through in time and this was why his psychiatric appointment at mental hygiene for the following morning at eight o'clock was never honored. I know for a fact that it had been called in and had been set up on a second priority. First priority is for an emergency but second priority should take precedence over all else. Such is the nature of things coming out of Special Inquiries and the cage. Ultimately they dropped the AWOL charges against him and processed him for his psychiatric discharge in the midst of a lot of confusion.

On July 15, 1971, I went down to see for myself how, and/or if, conditions had improved. I was met at the Fort Dix bus station by an Army car and taken to the Public Relations office. Then I was driven over to PCF. At first sight I was bowled over by the dramatic change. The barracks were newly painted, all the men were wearing uniforms. There were no bodies slumped over the front steps; no shattered glass as far as the eye could see.

Colonel Moon, a tall, bright, energetic, ambitious officer who had recently been appointed commander of the control facility, was eager to discuss the improvements in PCF, and feeling that I might consider his version biased, he called a Sergeant William R. Vaughan, a systems analyst. Both Colonel Moon and Sergeant Vaughan had served time in Vietnam. The Sergeant declared that when he was first faced with PCF duty, "I felt I was back in Vietnam without a weapon," but that now things are a whole lot better. "Now it's a decent place to live. In my opinion, it's just improved a hundred percent. One of the main reasons for individuals going AWOL in the past has been the conditions existing here. And now if an individual leaves PCF it's not because of conditions or his treatment here. It's within the individual."

Colonel Moon was very defensive about the minority group problems. He himself is black. Sergeant Vaughan is white and as eager to please Colonel Moon as Colonel Moon is to improve PCF. When in our discussion the Sergeant stumbled onto the minority problem in terms of percentage, Colonel Moon was unhappy about it. He was ignorant of the background, of the troubles Tim Coulter reported in PCF back in the days when it was known as SPD.

Colonel Moon had been the deputy inspector at Fort Dix in 1966. He had been the Equal Employment officer at Dix and had been an advisor in Vietnam in the city of Hué during the Communist Tet offensive in 1968. The past three years he had spent as Deputy Comptroller at Fort Dix.

He was not surprised that he was called to PCF when things got rough. He didn't volunteer for the job. He said: "I can tell you I heard it yesterday from the Deputy Company Commander—this is the toughest job in the Army (PCF). It's the toughest job in the Army primarily because of the high turnover of people and the high density of people. I'd say roughly eleven hundred people. We have about two hundred and forty-five in the stockade. Our strength here is going up, so it's about, say, two hundred and thirty right here and then there'll be about one hundred up at the 1387 which is the rehabilitation platoon. There's a number of people on excess leave. Excess leave means that if a man is awaiting a board action, and it looks like the chances are very likely that it will be approved, there is no longer any need to keep the man here. We say to him, ok, you are free to go on excess leave. He comes back periodically and he checks on the status of his discharge. Right now, in PCF, in this facility, there's about two hundred twenty-five [on excess leave]. I'd like to get the figures down to a manageable level. If we were trying to handle eleven hundred people physically that would be very tough. You don't ever want to get to where you're holding those large numbers of people."

When asked about the cage he said: "I thought many times about taking it down but very frankly, I'll tell you that it can't come down. It just cannot. And the reason why it cannot come down is that these men are brought in from the first precinct in New York City and they're brought in on the bus. They're under complete restraint all the way until they get here. Now obviously, if you took those men off the bus and you just turned them loose without any restraint, it would present quite a problem. We hope to keep the men there no more than three hours. Our processing cycle's the whole thing that this is geared to.

"Let's say that a man has an antisocial problem here. In order to get to the stockade he goes over there to the holding area [cage] temporarily until the confinement orders can be typed up and he can be issued the proper clothes to go to the stockade and then he is escorted to post-confinement facilities.

"Civilians who have turned themselves in also come through the holding area [cage]. Matter of fact, most of our people turn themselves in voluntarily to the Provost Marshal here at Fort Dix. Then they come to us. I don't expect the public to understand this kind of thing, but this is the system and the system has to be geared this way. There's just no way of getting around it. I'll tell you frankly that we did have one guard who was hurt while I was thinking about pulling that area down. You see the problem is, you've got to understand, we've got thirty or forty human beings there who are tensed up. You put them in a room and you put one guard in there with them, and you can't protect that man. Really what that thing [cage] does is sort of channels them into one area to come out the gate. That was the only reason for the thing [cage] in the first place. Now what you have to do, I think, you have to make sure that this thing [cage] isn't used for anything else other than the purposes I have said. Because one thing that I don't want to build here is the image that we are a confinement facility. We're not a confinement facility. You want to see somebody who confines somebody, you've got to go to the post stockade. This is not the area here."

Colonel Moon asked Sergeant William R. Vaughan to carry on. Sergeant Vaughan:

"When I first arrived here, this was a pretty sad situation; and Colonel Moon, at the beginning he started initiating programs for better improvement, improving the processing of the individuals and the systems involved there. He initiated a scientific approach to solving these operations procedures in order to speed up processing of the individual. Work simplification; this is the scientific approach to identifying problems and analysing it and determining the best solution to the problem. Also, Colonel Moon felt that he should have a good understanding of the individuals here in order to deal with them effectively, such as all the characteristics of their background and things of this nature and we have a complete report here of the individuals such as where their home state of residency, their race, age, and things of this nature."

I asked Colonel Moon about the people who don't speak English.

Colonel Moon: "They always find a Puerto Rican who can speak Spanish."

I asked if the non-English speaking soldiers shouldn't be mustered out immediately.

Colonel Moon: "I have no authority."

I asked who did.

Colonel Moon: "Nobody does once he's joined the service, really, and he's inducted. There are some other ways this sort of thing can be handled. I think you realize that just a few years ago we used to have English-speaking classes for people and I'm sure that these classes are still conducted in the Army, but that's not my business. I have nothing to do with that."

Sergeant Vaughan: "Also, we determined that according to the present, if things continue the way they have been, based on 1970, that we would have a fourteen percent increase in incoming personnel over the next two years. Due to the programs that Colonel Moon has initiated here and the overall improvement of PCF we have reduced this by three and a half percent. First of all, just making this a better living place for individuals. The improvement of the treatment of the casuals, of better understanding of their problems and making more effort to solve their problems for them; taking a genuine interest in the individual."

Colonel Moon: "In other words, greater numbers of people were hanging around to get their discharges taken care of, rather than going right back out again."

Sergeant Vaughan: "And also, this three and a half percent has been a reduction since Colonel Moon has taken over and now we have a twenty-five percent reduction in the month of July for the first thirteen days as compared to June. This is twenty-three percent improvement over last year. And so all indications are that we're on the right road here."

I asked about whether there were ample eating utensils now.

Colonel Moon: "That doesn't seem much of a problem. That has reduced itself but I think I'd say the same thing to you I said to Mr. Larry Jackson, there has to be a certain amount of motivation that comes from the individual himself. These men live together. They live in the barracks. They are even required during the week to have certain of their buddies watch their gear. But you know there is a problem of loyalty among them. What I'm really saying is they have to do something themselves to come forward, stand up and be counted and say, 'This guy took my stuff.' Because many times since I've been here, these things occur with people right within the barracks."

I asked about whether each man had a uniform now.

Colonel Moon: "Yes, they have uniforms. We have adequate wall lockers but they don't need them because they don't have that much stuff. One set or possibly two sets of digs, that's it. What I don't want anybody to do is get to the point that they *like* this place so well that they want to stay here."

Asked about the drug problem, Colonel Moon answered:
"Has it increased or decreased? We don't know. Detoxification? If a PCFer is going into withdrawal symptoms, he can go to the hospital and it's up to the medical authorities there to determine the appropriate action. If he wants to turn himself in and kick the habit, he can turn himself in to the Drug Amnesty program which was instituted by the Commander General, in late May or early June. Now if you ask me if that has any im-

mediate effect on me, I'll tell you no, it doesn't mean a thing. They [PCFers] want to check the place out, but once they found no methadone there, they backed away.

"I don't agree with methadone as a solution. Because all it does is put you on another form—take them off morphine, put them on heroin, now they are taking them off heroin, and putting them on methadone. I don't like the fact that my men are using drugs; I don't like that fact and I'll say it very loud and clear. If I catch a man shooting drugs in my barracks he's going to the stockade. It's as simple as that. Why? Because he becomes a potential contaminator of everybody else. If I catch the culprit, if I catch him pushing drugs, yes, I'm going to punish him. Don't ask me if I'm going to put him into the medical rehabilitation program. Tell him to see somebody else. That's not my job here, as the commander of this facility. It's my responsibility to give them as good a facility as I can under the limiting practices that we have here. I've got a simple rule: If you're going to shoot, don't shoot in my area. Because if you do, don't ask me if I'm going out there and put the soldier through some big Rockefeller program. I don't have any facilities for that. That's not my concern. This man is here to have his problems resolved and these problems are between him and the Army because of AWOL. He's not here because of drug addiction. That just happens to be a side effect of what goes on. Now, if a man needs help, I will refer him to the appropriate facilities, but my job stops right there, when I refer him to the facility.

"Three-quarters of the stockade comes from the PCF, because the biggest problem is the AWOL problem."

Colonel Moon asked Sergeant Vaughan to continue.

Sergeant Vaughan: "Would you like to start with the characteristics of some of their backgrounds? We have this broken down percentage-wise."

Colonel Moon: "I'm not necessarily interested in those because what I am a little bit concerned about here is that what she [the author] writes goes to the American public. I'm not interested in making any slurs between any ethnic groups. If we come out with the percentages that are Puerto Rican percentages or black—that's going to turn a lot of people in the wrong direction."

I suggested that this was already known.

Colonel Moon: "Well, I would prefer that you didn't get that from me. Your story is centered on the American public.

My concern is the welfare of my men and I don't want any sort of stigmatism attached to the job. They're hassled enough already as it is. Now if you want to say that the masses of these people are minority people yes, they are, and that's not going to help anything. Because first of all it just happened that way. There's a reason for it, and the reason for it is that minority groups congregate in one place in the city and they're very easily picked up because they go to Joe's Joint and they stand around and they profile and the man's got them. The other guy, the Caucasian guy for example, he can walk home. He can get lost in the crowd, into his own environment. That's why it has nothing to do with the Army. It's just that these guys are picked up. And the other thing, they have a tendency to stick around here more than the other fellows. Every man who comes in through the holding area is dealt with appropriately. I don't think these statistics of the racial component in PCF help at all."

"My prediction is that the input will reduce. As the efficiency increases, our monthly input will drop instead of continuing at the same level. Why do I say that? Because a large number of the people that we handle here are repeaters. Let me give you an example. You are worried about what's going to happen to you in your own individual case. If I can take you to the point where you get to court and the court gives you your punishment, then you're just waiting around for shipment. You're not up-tight any more, because you're not worried about what's going to happen. It's already come and it's already gone. We've made a tremendous change in personnel. I just lifted out everyone, as many people as I could and put different people in. I wanted the best the post had. I asked for that. Sergeant Vaughan, Major Endicott, Sergeant Arthur and me, I like to think we're top notch people.

"I like people. I have a tremendous respect for them, I've always had it, and I never had any problems with any of the people I've commanded or controlled because I vibrate that kind of feeling. There's one thing I'll say about the fellows in here, particularly the northeasterner—he's the man we're dealing with primarily, these guys can see a phony in a minute. They know where they stand. I see the fellows go to the stockade—they don't even get mad at me going to the stockade because they know, every guy gets a chance. The guys that are over there, they deserve to be there. If a soldier has a short-term AWOL he's *not going to the stockade.* He's coming out here. He's free. Now I've got one policy and that is if he goes

AWOL from here, if I've got room in the stockade when he comes back, he's going in. It's as simple as that, because I want to stop this foolishness of running back and forth."

At the end of my visit in PCF I walked inside the barracks and the conditions were improved, latrines and all. Colonel Moon suggested that I talk to the men without his presence and I got varied reactions, from: "A lot of changes. The system's run differently" to, "You kidding? There ain't no fixin' can be done to this place!" I spoke to men who had spent three and four days in the cage and to men who claimed things were speeded up and only if you were going into the stockade would you spend more than a day in the cage.

Finally a picture of how it all seemed in May, 1971, to writers on FRAGGING ACTION, the Fort Dix underground paper that took over when SHAKEDOWN discontinued: "LIFERS PUT ON A CIRCUS IN AWOLLAND":

> Fort Dix's Special Processing Battalion (now known as PCF) is where returned AWOL EM [enlisted men] wait out the grinding gears of "military justice." (Unless they're put in jail before they're tried.) SPB recently had a rash of visitors, beginning with Congressman Dellums of California and ending with the CONARC commander, a 4-star-general. Also a lot of reporters, from the Trentonian to a CBS news team with cameras.

> For a couple of weeks the local brass ran around like chickens with their heads cut off, in a panicky effort to cover up the real conditions that EM [Enlisted Men] are living [sic] in there.

> At SPB the brass "process," every month, up to 1000 or more AWOL GIs who were busted or turned themselves in around the N.Y.-N.J. area. These are among the hundreds of thousands throughout the Army each year who are saying "shove it" to military life, or to the Vietnam war, and going AWOL. At SPB they wait for weeks or months for assembly-line punishment from the brass, who don't recognize that the Army is the problem which causes AWOLs, not the individual GI. The Army makes no effort whatsoever to deal with the problems that made EM go AWOL. The brass throws them in the stockade, or takes away their pay, or sends them back to some duty as bad or worse than they had before.

ON THE SCRAPHEAP

Meanwhile, while these GIs are at SPB they're jammed into the run-down, pre-World War II wooden buildings that still pass for barracks. Most of these barracks have serious defects, such as the plumbing, that are never really repaired. They are condemned by common agreement even of the brass, but they're used anyway. Unlike other buildings of the same type on Ft. Dix, they have been neither torn down nor renovated. A lot of the guys go AWOL again from SPB because they can't take the conditions here. Even so, the barracks are overcrowded, and the brass have to keep a large portion of the men assigned there on pass or excess leave.

SPB is the military's ghetto: a place where living conditions are miserable, the housing goes unrepaired by the "landlords," and necessary services are denied to the people who live there. Much of the population of SPB is black and Puerto Rican, from the cities of N.Y. and N.J., people who have enough economic burdens at home without the Army on their backs as well. By contrast, the interviewing officers who decide who will go to the stockade are all white, at the moment.

There are serious problems here, people who have lived under terrific oppression. Problems of economic hardship, of individuals and families; problems of heroin and other drugs. But the brass deals with SPB from a police point of view, and go on giving out punishment for the length and repetition of AWOLs. They have no counselors and no programs that could begin to deal with such problems. The Army got what it could out of these men, and now it has thrown them just as easily on the trash pile.

THE SIDESHOW

When the generals and the press came, it was unbelievable how the local commanders ran around trying to change everything in a few days, or else cover it up. One of the barracks, the 4th platoon, was shut down and locked because it couldn't be made even halfway decent looking for the higher ups. It was all right for the brass to keep men in that barracks for months, but they were suddenly afraid to let their "superiors" see it. All in one or two days, the barracks got new mattresses, new wall lockers, new paint, and hurry-up repairs. At the "cage," a fenced room where the AWOLs are confined on the first day they arrive, all at once there was new paint, pictures on the walls, mirrors in the nearest latrine, a water fountain that worked (it never had before), and a TV set! (That was removed afterwards.) None of those things had ever been there before. Outside, softball equipment suddenly appeared.

In the afternoon following the visit of the general, the XO of HQ Comd (Special Troops), LTC Crozhier, was personally giving life-type haircuts to the prisoners in the cage. We doubt if he's a licensed barber, as the AR's are supposed to guarantee.

The officer in charge of inprocessing moved twenty or thirty guys out of the cage when the general was there. They went to the baggage section, where they supposedly were getting clothing, but they spent the whole afternoon. Probably he was hiding them so the cage wouldn't look so crowded. This same ILT lied to a reporter that no one stayed in the cage overnight, which is actually a common practice.

What anyone can see is that the Army has no solutions for the problems of SPB, no help for guys with real problems that made them go AWOL. The Army just punishes them or gives them Undesirable Discharges, which may cause more problems back home, like unemployment. The large number of AWOLs is no excuse for lack of legal protection, but how can your rights be protected at SPB where you stand in line for summary court-martials that take a few minutes?

SPB will probably go back to its normal, miserable condition in a short time, since the main concern of the brass is their own skins. They won't change anything, unless it's to come down harder on the AWOL GIs. Not being able to put up with those lifers is what makes most guys go AWOL in the first place. The EM [enlisted man] may not put up with it forever.

I thought I had come to the end of the bestial conditions at Dix, of the physical filth, of the skid row living conditions, but I was mistaken.

On August 12, 1971 I went down to the Military Law Project which has continued the work of The Coffeehouse, but on a more professional basis. Essentially, it helps servicemen with their legal problems and teaches servicemen to help each other in counseling men who have had erroneous induction or want CO discharges or, as in the case of a young veteran I met there (who had been shot through the head and out one ear in Vietnam and was deaf in this one ear), to get a medical discharge.

I was talking to two young soldiers, Private William F. Caron and Private Scott Thomas and they were describing the ghastly conditions in which they were living and how they had never dreamed that the Army of the USA would allow such squalor, how they had both been "gung ho" to start with and now were totally turned off. They were helping the Center and were writing and editing FRAGGING ACTION. In my naïveté I said, "Oh, you mean PCF." No, they said, they were living in "STC." I suggested that perhaps the initials had been changed again and that we were talking about the same place. I was wrong. "STC" (Special Training Company) is not the area where returning AWOL soldiers are billeted but is the area in which the men who cannot keep up to Basic Training are housed. I was told that there were three sections in STC. One section for people who can't speak English and can't read on a fifth-grade level; another section for people who simply cannot keep up in Basic—not because of physical deformities, but because they are too fat or skinny or simply too slow, and the third section called "Profiles." This section consists of people who came into the Army with something drastically wrong with them but didn't realize it.

Scott Thomas said: "If you can still walk with crutches they keep you in the Army. If your eyesight is bad but you are not totally blind, if you're a borderline medical discharge and the hospital won't give you the discharge, you get thrown in STC. There are guys who have infections in their bones and they can hardly walk in STC. In my opinion they should give them a choice like if you stay in we'll try and help you become physically fit or if we can't we'll discharge you. But instead they send you to STC where they ignore your condition. Men who have suffered serious injuries in Basic Training are thrown in STC. There are about 400 men in STC."

Private Caron told me that he had "varicoseles," a varicose vein in one of his testicles.

"I knew there was something wrong with me before I came

into the Army, but because I didn't have the money I never checked into it. When I went into Basic Training I started to get a very bad pain down there so I went to sick call and they told me I had Varicoseles. They gave me a profile for ninety days. I went to a JAG officer and he said, 'Yeah, you should be discharged. The Army doesn't want to give it to you. What can I do?' "

Private Caron told me that he had been ordered on his hands and knees to paint the floor in the latrine.

"It was so dirty you couldn't get the dirt off. We painted over dead cockroaches. The sinks would be covered with bugs. We have no laundry facilities. The gutters and the whole side of the building is tearing off from the foundation. I wouldn't let a dog live there. I tried to get the guys to do something about the conditions but their attitude was: Forget it, we'll only be here another week. But I don't feel that way about it. Other people are going to have to live there. I don't just care about me."

The saddest case I heard about was Dean Friscano who was in the stockade and had been a close friend of Scot and Williams. Dean had campaigned for Senator McCarthy. He had been drafted from Monroe Community College though he had applied for a Conscientious Objector status. In his application he had declared: "I am totally against wars in which human life is wasted on political ideologies and nationalistic disputes." He refused to train with a gun in Basic. They shipped him to a clerk's school and to a cook's school. He kept trying for a discharge for psychiatric reasons. He was very high strung and upset. Dr. Harry Murphy, a Major in the Army, recommended that he be given a discharge on psychiatric grounds. The commanding officer refused to grant it.

Dean was sent to Fort Sill in April 1971, but when he told them that he had never completed Basic, never fired a weapon, they sent him back to Dix to STC. He went AWOL for two weeks but on returning was put in STC not PCF. He was ordered to have a haircut which he did but was then told it wasn't short enough, though it was regulation length. Dean had no money left for another haircut and he refused. He was sent to the stockade for hard labor and 45 days. William Caron then told us the rest of Dean's story: "Last week, last Thursday a friend told me that he'd seen him [Dean] in the emergency ward of the hospital, that Dean couldn't speak. He was hand-cuffed with a guard. My friend tried to find out what happened and Dean was trying to get the words out but just couldn't talk. Finally the guard told my friend that Dean had tried to commit suicide by tying his socks together and hanging himself and then by slitting his wrists. I was very upset because Dean was a close friend and a great guy, so thanks to a friendly guard, two of us got into the stockade. We were taken to Dean's solitary cell. Dean was sleeping. When he woke up he didn't recognize us."

Though the war may have ended overseas, we have made our own darkness at noon here at home. Countless young men of conscience who don't have pull, money or connections remain caged in silence and filth. They write letters to their congressmen, they cry out in the underground papers. They can't break free from the bars of official indifference, the cage of official injustice.

ABOUT THE AUTHOR

Joan Crowell, a free-lance writer, poet and novelist, lives in Manhattan with her second husband, David G. Crowell. The mother of five grown children, she received her B.A. from Bennington College and her M.A. from New York University where she taught in the English department. A former business manager of *Partisan Review*, she is currently executive director of the American Friends of Danilo Dolci. Under the name of Joan Simon, her works include articles in *Life*, *Ramparts*, *The Nation*, *Commonweal*, a poem in *New York Quarterly*, a novel, *Portrait of a Father*, and two original opera librettos. She is currently at work on a trilogy of novels set in New York City.